THE HAITIAN REVOLUTION

CELEBRATING THE FIRST BLACK REPUBLIC

by Charles L. Blockson

THE
DONNING COMPANY
PUBLISHERS

The Donning Company Publishers
184 Business Park Drive, Suite 206
Virginia Beach, VA 23462

Steve Mull, General Manager
Barbara B. Buchanan, Office Manager
Pamela Koch, Editor
Lori Wiley, Senior Graphic Designer
Stephanie Danko, Imaging Artist
Mary Ellen Wheeler, Proofreader
Anne Cordray, Project Research Coordinator
Scott Rule, Director of Marketing
Travis Gallup, Marketing Coordinator

Mary Taylor, Project Director

Library of Congress Cataloging-in-Publication Data

Blockson, Charles L.
   The Haitian Revolution : celebrating the first black republic / by Charles L. Blockson.
      p. cm.
   Includes bibliographical references.
   ISBN 1-57864-272-8 (soft cover : alk. paper)
1. Haiti--History--Revolution, 1791-1804--Anniversaries, etc.--Exhibitions.
2. Slavery--Haiti--History--Exhibitions. 3. Haiti--History--Pictorial works--Exhibitions. I. Title.
 F1923.B665 2004
 972.94'0074'74811--dc22
                                    2004011125

Printed in the United States of America at Walsworth Publishing Company

INTRODUCTION

The Haitian Revolution: Celebrating the First Black Republic, with Charles L. Blockson serving as guest curator, examines the Haitian rebellion, a critical juncture in world history whose significance resonated beyond its natural boundaries as a victory for the fundamental ideals of liberty and equality. The exhibition offers vivid artistic illustrations, as well as accurate historical accounts of the struggles of enslaved Africans to be free. It is not a popular, sanitized, or politically safe version of history.

The Haitian liberation is a source of great hope, admiration, and pride for all oppressed people throughout the world because the Haitians overthrew their oppressors, thus eliminating the socioeconomic structure of greed and brutality upon which slavery was constructed. The seeds of the Haitian uprising began in 1791 when Boukman, a Voodoo priest and an early organizer of the Revolution, led successful attacks with his enslaved African comrades against white plantation owners. Toussaint L'Ouverture with freedom fighters Jean-Jacques Dessalines, Henri Christophe, Marie-Jeanne Lamartiniere, and countless others participated in the defeat of the world's greatest military force, the French Army of Napoleon Bonaparte, during the late eighteenth century.

Through rare books, paintings, documents, sculpture, and other objects primarily from the Charles L. Blockson Afro-American Collection at Temple University, *The Haitian Revolution: Celebrating the First Black Republic* consciously places the extraordinary story of the Haitian Revolution at the center of freedom and liberation struggles in the annals of modern history. The exhibition also displays collections of The African American Museum in Philadelphia. Vibrant paintings by internationally renowned Haitian artist Ulrick Jean-Pierre heighten the visual narrative. *The Haitian Revolution* offers the museum an opportunity to explore the evolution of the Haitian Republic, as well as to interpret cultural expressions emanating from the African Diaspora.

Although the significance of the first modern Black republic is mired in literary obscurity, *The Haitian Revolution: Celebrating the First Black Republic* presents this historical event as one of the greatest military accomplishments in world history. Many publications about the Haitian Revolution are condescending in tone, and oftentimes disregard or diminish the historical significance of Haiti's successful liberation from slavery. Eagerly removing the stigma of the Haitian Revolution from a remote analysis, the exhibition takes a fresh perspective that highlights the radical thinking and superior military tactics of Toussaint L'Ouverture. The exhibition investigates the causes and the effects of slavery. It examines little known but important historical facts, from the Haitians who participated in the American Revolution to the Haitian Revolution and its aftermath, as well as how the African victory during their freedom struggle became a serious threat to slaveholders in the Western Hemisphere, especially those plantation owners in the southeastern region of the United States and Cuba. Severe paranoia erupted in the United States after the Haitian Revolution and white southerners' attitudes changed toward enslaved Africans. The Haitian Revolution accentuated African resistance to slavery. Speculation suggests a strong parallel between the Denmark Vesey revolt in South Carolina and the Haitian conflict because of Vesey's attempts to communicate with Haiti for support of his revolt.

From the nineteenth century through the twenty-first century, influential figures such as Frederick Douglass, Marcus Garvey, Zora Neale Hurston, Barbara Jordan, Amiri Baraka, Danny Glover, and Randall Robinson have admired the Haitian Revolution as the first example of Black freedom in the Western Hemisphere. After two hundred years of liberation, *The Haitian Revolution: Celebrating the First Black Republic* is a testimony to the importance of the Haitian Revolution, which continues to shine brightly as a beacon of hope to all who cherish and are willing to fight for freedom.

Harry Harrison
President and CEO
The African American Museum in Philadelphia

ORIGIN

This exhibit, *The Haitian Revolution: Celebrating the First Black Republic*, presents an overview of the long and turbulent history of Haiti from 1492 to 2004. Through books, broadsides, coins, paintings, prints, photographs, postcards, pamphlets, sculptures, manuscripts, newspapers, and other historical documents, the exhibit seeks to educate the viewer about the sources of pride in a rich Haitian heritage. The exhibition is divided into a number of parts that trace the story of Haiti through many developments, from the unspeakable horror of enslavement to the present-day turmoil in Haiti.

In the pages of the catalogue and in the exhibit, the viewer will meet and come to know major and unknown personalities in this dramatic chapter in Haitian history. Brave men and women served their country well. Included among the men were Toussaint L'Ouverture, Jean-Jacques Dessalines, Henri Christophe, and Charlemagne Peralte. Women such as Zabeth risked their lives by escaping from the sugar plantations. In spite of the chains, the red-hot poker, and the leg irons that Zabeth was forced to endure, she escaped many times until, at the age of twenty, she died within the walls of the fort sugar mill in Leogane in western Haiti. Dessalines honored Marie-Jeanne Lamartiniere for her courage during one of Haiti's important battles of the Revolution while Catherine Flond sewed the Haitian flag after Dessalines tore the white out of the French flag. Defilee gathered the body parts of Emperor Dessalines after his assassination. These and other significant events are fully treated through the more than two hundred items on display.

What would have been the fate of the United States of America had there been no Haiti? The story of Haiti's all-black regiment's participation in the American Revolutionary War against British tyrannical rule for independence is one of the neglected aspects of American history. However, when the Haitians fought for their own independence through the slave revolt of 1791 that led to the first black republic in the Western Hemisphere, many of America's founding fathers looked upon the Haitian freedom fighters with disdain. The Haitian people are still paying the price for gaining their freedom two hundred years ago. In October 2002, more than two hundred Haitian immigrants arrived in Miami, Florida, on small boats. They were arrested by police officers, restrained, handcuffed, placed in vehicles, and transported to Krome Detention Center in West Miami where they were held for a long period.

In August 2004, the most singular triumph of the Haitian Bicentennial is being commemorated with a cruise to Haiti—Cruising Into History. This pilgrimage to an International Black Arts and Cultural Festival was organized by Ron Daniels, founder/chairman, Haiti Support Project, and a large group of prominent African Americans including Danny Glover, ambassador-at-large, and Philadelphia's own, Councilwoman Jannie L. Blackwell and C. DeLores Tucker.

As curator of this exhibition, I had the unique task of selecting each item, as well as writing the text and captions of the catalogue. The majority of items on display are from the Charles L. Blockson Afro-American Collection, Temple University, supplemented by unique items from my private collection. Other items are from the private art collection of The African American Museum of Philadelphia and the private art collections of Paul and Laura Keene, the Jerome family, Diane Turner, and Picard and Sharon Losier. The exhibition and my role as guest curator would not be possible had it not been for the great generosity of Harry Harrison, president and CEO of The African American Museum of Philadelphia.

Many thanks to Lisa Fitch, my administrative specialist, for typing the catalogue text and captions. In addition, I would like to thank Dr. Diane Turner, Richard Watson, Leslie Willis, John Waites, and other staff members of The African American Museum in Philadelphia. They all did an immense amount of work assembling the exhibit. I wish to express my particular appreciation to the following people for their support: Councilwoman Jannie L. Blackwell and Mary Bomar, superintendent, Independence National Historical Park for their generous donations, Sacaree Rhodes, Generations Unlimited,

Mrs. Delores Mohammed, Dr. Cecile Accilien, Ulrick Jean-Pierre, Nate Clark, the LaRose family, Louis Massiah, Phyllis Morales, and my daughter Noelle Blockson for her complete support. Finally, I extend a heartfelt salute to all Haitians within the African Diaspora. With great respect and with enduring affection, this exhibition, *The Haitian Revolution: Celebrating the First Black Republic*, is your contribution to America.

The exhibition is on display beginning May 7, 2004.

Charles L. Blockson
February 2004

AFRICAN WARRIOR

FROM FREEDOM TO SLAVERY

"MOTHER AFRICA"—THE HAITIANS' HOMELAND

Africa's cultural heritage is as old as humankind itself. For it is in Africa that the oldest known human fossils and artifacts have been unearthed. Much of Africa's traditional literature and history is oral; however, people of African descent have written in various languages on almost every conceivable subject, from as early as 1000 A.D., some three hundred years before the Mohammedans invaded Africa.

The kings of the Ashanti people in Ghana sat on thrones encased in massive gold, were enveloped in the richest silks, and wore as many ornaments of pure gold around their necks, arms, wrists, fingers, and ankles as they comfortably could. In the Western Sudanese civilizations, Mali, a highly developed kingdom, attracted tradesmen and scholars throughout the ancient world, seeking knowledge at the University of Sankore located in the fabled city of Timbuktu. In the ancient city of Benin in Nigeria, Africa's largest country, for more than five hundred years, artists created objects in brass, ivory, terracotta, and wood for use in divine kingship and queenship rituals. These objects adorned the royal palaces to honor the king and queen mothers, chiefs, warriors, and other prominent officials of the court. Then came the Ewe kingdom of Dahomey, a large and rich state with a considerable army, constitutionally very complex, and governed by kings and queens who were often excellent rulers. Nzinga (1582–1663), famous Amazon queen of Matamba, West Africa, led her army of fierce women warriors against the Portuguese and other European slave traders. She won battle after battle. Other African rulers continued to repel invading European slave hunters for centuries.

MAP OF SAINT-DOMINGUE, 1797

THE TERROR OF ENSLAVEMENT

English historian Basil Davidson wrote, "Between the 15th and 19th centuries, the African continent earned the name 'Black Mother' because of its seemingly inexhaustible supply of humanity to work the mines and plantations of the Western Hemisphere" (*Black Mother, The Years of African Slave Trade: Precolonial History 1450–1850*, 1961). The European international slave trade led to what scholar Walter Rodney documented as the "underdevelopment of Africa." The traffic

7

AFRICAN MOTHER AND CHILD

in human beings for profitable purposes introduced a culture of violence that began in Africa and crossed the Atlantic Ocean to the colonies where enslaved Africans were brutally forced to work against their will. The enslavement of Africans was a brutal process—levels of systematic terrorism—that included mechanisms in the slavocracy to ensure that enslaved Africans' labor was exploited and that they were denied basic rights as human beings, from birth to death, or escape from slavery.

On the coasts of Africa where enslaved Africans were held, sometimes for months at a time, they were taken in chains, from dungeons at night, through the Door of No Return to the holds of ships. European slave ships took many weeks to traverse the Atlantic Ocean during the Middle Passage—the horrible one-way journey—the distance between Africa and the New World of Haiti, other Caribbean islands, and the Americas. During the voyage, enslaved Africans died from overcrowding and diseases, while others out of fear and melancholy committed suicide by jumping overboard in the shark-infested oceans. They were chained together, given food that was spoiled and often unfit to digest, as well as stagnant water. C.L.R. James noted that: "Fear of their cargo bred a savage cruelty in the crew. One captain, to strike terror into the rest, killed a slave and dividing heart, liver, and entrails into 300 pieces made each of the slaves eat one, threatening those who refused with the same torture" (*Black Jacobins,* 1989, 9).

For enslaved Africans, newly arrived and huddled in fright in Haiti, all they had was each other, their memories of the communities they were forced to leave, and a burning desire for freedom. In their state of terror as well as the tremendous burden of bondage, their quest was not only to survive but also to escape the oppressive condition of slavery.

EXPLORATION AND DOMINATION

When Christopher Columbus arrived in "Ayti," translated "land of high mountains," on December 6, 1492, searching for gold, the island was inhabited by more than one million natives, the Taino Indians of the Arawak tribe. Columbus named the island Hispaniola, and it became Spain's

first colony in the Western Hemisphere. Within thirty years of Columbus's arrival, the original inhabitants had virtually disappeared through disease, involuntary hard labor, slaughter, and suicide. Some managed to escape to the mountains and set up secret encampments. The Spanish replaced the Taino with Carib Indians, who also died or escaped from their harsh treatment. At the beginning of the sixteenth century, the Spanish brought West Africans as slaves to the island.

The Spanish began to abandon Hispaniola because no rich deposits of gold had been found.

By 1697, Spain ceded the western third of the island to the French who were not searching for gold but colonies to produce lucrative crops like sugar and cotton. The French named their new colony Saint Dominique. With the labor of enslaved West Africans, the French established a flourishing slave plantation system throughout the colony. By the end of the next century, Saint Dominique (the French colonial term for Hayti) was the world's richest colony.

By 1791, the "Pearl of the Antilles" produced 60 percent of the world's coffee and 40 percent of its sugar. This level of production translated into hard labor and pain for enslaved Africans, who were worked like animals. The enslavement of Africans and the maintenance of slavery required the harshest punishments. Whipping was authorized through the Negro Code in 1685. Any punishment that required more than one hundred lashes was handed over to the authorities, but enslaved Africans were regularly whipped to death. There were different types of whips: from an ordinary cane to woven cord to *rigoise* (a thick thong of cowhide) to *lianes* (local growths of reeds, supple and pliant like whalebone) (*Black Jacobins*, 12). James noted "slaves received the whip with more certainty and regularity than they received their food. It was the incentive to work and the guardian of discipline" (*Black Jacobins*, 12).

Enslaved Africans faced many types of torture by the whip. James noted "a thousand

ENSLAVED WOMEN BEING TERRORIZED UNDER FRENCH RULE

refinements" with special names from the "four-post" (where enslaved Africans were tied to four posts on the ground) to "the torture of the ladder" (where enslaved Africans were tied to ladders) to "the hammock" (where enslaved Africans' limbs were suspended). In the case of a pregnant woman who received the "four-post" whip technique, a hole was dug in the ground for the unborn child (*Black Jacobins,* 13).

On the eve of the Haitian Revolution, three social groups populated the island: white colonists, free people of African descent, and enslaved Africans. The island's population at that time consisted of more than 450,000 enslaved Africans, about 30,000 white French planters, and more than 25,000 biracial free people who formed an important class in Saint Dominique society. These gens de couleur, or mulattos of African and French descent, were called sacatra, grifle, Affranchis, jaune, quateron, and many other names depending on the portion of their African and European ancestry. A number of these individuals were wealthy landowners and slaveholders themselves. The free blacks were initially tolerated by the white population of Saint Dominique but did not enjoy full citizenship rights. Each group had political goals. Most of the whites wanted self-government. Free people of color wanted equality with whites. Enslaved Africans wanted their freedom. When the slave revolt began, free people of color joined the enslaved African people of the island and fought against the French inhabitants of Saint Dominique.

ITEMS ON DISPLAY

Christopher Columbus/Print/Courtesy Charles L. Blockson Afro-American Collection, Temple University

Early map of Saint Dominique/Courtesy Charles L. Blockson Afro-American Collection, Temple University

Arawak Indians—Original inhabitants of Haiti/Prints/Courtesy Charles L. Blockson Afro-American Collection, Temple University

African warrior and African mother and child/Color lithograph poster print/Courtesy Charles L. Blockson Private Collection, Temple University

Depiction of enslavement on the island of Saint Dominique/Prints/ Courtesy Charles L. Blockson Private Collection, Temple University

Various African people dressed in their native clothing and representation of hairstyles/Hand color prints/Courtesy Charles L. Blockson Private Collection, Temple University

Igbo Man in Chains/Bronze Statue/Courtesy Charles L. Blockson Private Collection

Capitao Do Matto/Print/Courtesy of Charles L. Blockson Private Collection/Depiction of Spanish slave hunters and the capture of enslaved Africans in Saint Dominique

IGBO MAN IN CHAINS

Entrée du des Domingo/Courtesy Charles L. Blockson Afro-American Collection, Temple University/This early print shows a view of the port of entry during the time that the Spanish controlled the island known as St. Domingo.

Depiction of Africans carried off from West Africa to enslavement/Large color lithograph print/Courtesy Charles L. Blockson Afro-American Collection, Temple University

Moreau De Saint-Mery's Description Topographique, Phisique, Civile, Political, et Historique de la Parties Françoise de Isle Saint Dominique/Volume 1, Philadelphia, 1776/Courtesy Charles L. Blockson Afro-American Collection, Temple University

Marcus Rainsford's Historical Account of the Black Empire of Haiti/London, 1805/Courtesy Charles L. Blockson Afro-American Collection, Temple University

{*San Domingo*}: *Moreau de Saint-Mery M. De M. De Curt, Depute De La Guadeloupe au nom des Colonies Reunies, [with] opinion. De M. Moreau Des depute La Martinique Sur La Motion De M. Curt, Depute De La Guadeloupe, Pour L'Establissement D'un Comite Charge Particulierement De l'Examen de Tous Les Objets Coloniaux*/[caption] Paris 1789/Courtesy Charles L. Blockson Afro-American Collection, Temple University/The calling of the state general by King Louis XVI raised the question of how the colonies would be represented.

Apercu Sur La Constitution Des Saint Dominique, Paris, 1793/Courtesy Charles L. Blockson Afro-American Collection, Temple University/Marquis de Robert Nicolas Cocherel, a French captain and deputy from Saint Dominique,

DEPICTION OF AFRICANS CARRIED OFF FROM WEST AFRICA TO ENSLAVEMENT

argues for the virtual independence of the island, which he asserts is not a colony of France but culturally and historically speaking a separate province with a heterogeneous-speaking population, including the colored race "uprooted from Africa."

*Petition 1793—Petition Ampliative, En Faveur Des Blancs Et Des Noirs, Et Projet Duntraite Important Pour Les Colonies Et Pour L'état/*Courtesy Charles L. Blockson Afro-American Collection, Temple University/In 1685, France issued the Code Noir (Black Code) to control people of African descent in Saint Dominique.

*A Manuscript Sugar Inventory Listing Prices and Quantities of Various Types of Sugar from a West Indian Plantation 1690/*Courtesy Charles L. Blockson Afro-American Collection, Temple University/Michel Begon, a French colonial administrator, served in several Caribbean islands, first at Martinique and then at Saint Dominique.

*Sur Les Trouble De Saint Dominique—1798/*Courtesy Charles L. Blockson Afro-American Collection, Temple University/A pamphlet issued by a white colonist of Saint Dominique expresses uttermost concerns about the potential massacre of whites by the black population led by Toussaint L'Ouverture.

Julien Raymond L'Origine Et Les Progress Du Prejuge Des Colons Blanc Homme De Contre Les Hommes De Couleur, 1791/Courtesy Charles L. Blockson Private Collection/A strong petition to the French National Convention demanding equality for his countrymen.

*Loi—Portant Que Tout Homme Est Libre En France, et Que Guelle Soit Fa Couleur, Ilyjouit Lees Droits Decitogen, s'ilales qualities percrites par La Constitution. Donnée A' Paris, Les 16 Octobre 1791/*Courtesy Charles L. Blockson Afro-American Collection, Temple University/In an attempt to control persons of the African Diaspora in France and in their colonies, the French assembly on September 28, 1791, issued this decree at a time when African people were viewed as an increasing threat to the native white French population.

The Burning of Cap-Francais in Saint Dominique/Early print/Courtesy Charles L. Blockson Private Collection/ When Toussaint L'Ouverture heard of the planned invasion by Napoleon, he ordered his armies to burn the town and surrounding areas.

*Secret History: or the Horror of Saint Domingo in a Series of Letters, Written by a Lady at Cap-Francais to Colonel Burr, Late Vice President of the United States, Principally During the Command of General Rochambeau/*Philadelphia, 1808/Courtesy Charles L. Blockson Private Collection/Lenora Hassall of Philadelphia wrote this novel based on an eyewitness account of the upheaval in Saint Domingo. Sansay was an alleged mistress of Aaron Burr.

Map of Guadeloupe/Print/Courtesy Charles L. Blockson Afro-American Collection, Temple University/Guadeloupe, first colonized by the French in 1635, produced sugar cane for France for nearly three centuries thanks to the labor of enslaved Africans and their descendants. Unlike its counterpart in Haiti, the enslaved population of Guadeloupe reacted slowly to news of the French Revolution in 1789. No major revolt preceded the French Republic's abolition of slavery on February 4, 1794, although a series of isolated revolts in the towns of Ballief, Trois-Rivieres, and Ste. Anne contributed to the urgency of that decree. On November 29, 1802, three hundred enslaved Africans of Guadeloupe, led by the mulatto Delgres, leader of the armies of the republic, blew themselves up in a small mountain fortress, thus ending the slave rebellion of Guadeloupe.

Map of Martinique/Print/Courtesy Charles L. Blockson Afro-American Collection, Temple University/In 1640, during the reign of King Louis XIII, enslaved Africans were brought to Martinique for the first time, principally from Senegal, West Africa, to work in the sugar cane fields. The European international slave trade was presumably most active from 1722 to 1788. Some 600,000 slaves were forcibly displaced to the Caribbean on French ships.

In 1802, when news arrived in Martinique that Napoleon had restored slavery in Saint Dominique and Guadeloupe, several revolts broke out in Martinique before order was restored.

The History, Civil and Commercial of the British Colonies in the West Indies, London, 1794–1801/Courtesy Charles L. Blockson Afro-American Collection, Temple University/This edition provides a first-hand description of the Napoleonic War in the Caribbean including Haiti. Edwards was sent from England in his youth, succeeded to an estate there, and became a wealthy merchant.

A Summer on the Borders of the Caribbean Sea/J. Dennis Harris, 1861/Courtesy Charles L. Blockson Afro-American Collection, Temple University/This book, written in 1861 by J. Dennis Harris from Cleveland, Ohio, espoused on mass immigration of African Americans to the tropical region where black people outnumbered white people. Harris himself eventually joined a small colony in Haiti that had been founded by another African American, James T. Holly.

FORMS OF AFRICAN RESISTANCE TO SLAVERY

> *The difficulty was that though one could trap them like animals, transport them in pens, work them alongside an ass or a horse and beat both with the same stick, stable them and starve them, they remained, despite their black skins and curly hair, quite invincibly human beings, with the intelligence and resents of humans beings.*
>
> C.L.R. James, *The Black Jacobins*

Enslaved Africans in Haiti had grueling lives. They began work before dawn and often worked into the evening hours. Enslaved Africans responded to their inhumane conditions by inventing ways to resist, overtly and covertly, their enslavement. When their oppressors discovered resistance, the consequences were severe. C.L.R. James noted emergence of many brutal forms of punishments.

In spite of the terrorism used to keep enslaved Africans in their degraded status of "slave," Africans conducted many forms of resistance to their enslavement including running away, destroying crops, spontaneous and planned strikes, taking property, arson, attacks on whites, poisoning of slaveholders and their families, armed struggles, and the establishment of Maroons, as well as the retention of African traditions through dance, music, language patterns, moral narratives, and spiritual beliefs. The synthesis of traditional African religions and the imposition of Catholicism led to the development and practice of Voodoo by enslaved Africans as a major form of resistance to slavery. It was birthed from enslaved Africans' desires to preserve African traditions and culture, which became a vehicle for uniting people from different West African tribes. Their major objective was to unite to overthrow slavery.

THE SIGNIFICANCE OF VOODOO IN HAITIAN LIFE AND CULTURE

No exhibition pertaining to Haiti would be complete without mentioning the significance of the Vodun (Voodoo) religion; the Creole term is "Vodou," meaning "spirits." Two faces of faith, one African and the other Western, give Haitians the strength to survive bad times and worse. Inherited from West Africa, Voodoo is essentially a religion of the spirits. The term "Voodoo" is derived from the Fon (spoken in Benin) word "Vodu." The equivalent Yoruba term is "Orisha"; Yoruba is spoken in Nigeria, West Africa. Haitian belief acknowledges God as Gran Met, Creator of heaven and earth. From the mid-1600s, their French oppressors forbade enslaved Africans transported to Haiti to practice their ancestral religions. Forced to convert to Roman Catholicism, enslaved Africans never deserted their ancestral spirits but secretly worshipped them in the guise of Catholic saints.

Voodoo in Haitian history is a profound and unquestionable belief. The blue and red portions of the national flag represent Ogou, the Voodoo spirit of fire and war, and the cosmos; the red and black emblem symbolizes the Guedes, the Voodoo spirits of death. Every year on July 16, Haitians throughout the world return to Haiti to participate in the celebration of Vyej Mirak, an important religious ceremony where Christians and Voodooists worship together. Though 80 percent are Roman Catholics, Haitians remain deeply committed to Voodoo. In April 2003, President Jean-Bertrand Aristide's government officially sanctioned Voodoo as a religion, allowing practitioners to begin performing ceremonies ranging from baptisms to marriages with legal authority. In this display are gathered a number of masks, drums elaborately decorated, clothes, and wooden sculpture fetish figures associated with Voodoo ceremonies.

One of the primary purposes of this exhibition is to comprehensively record as much as possible the complete history and culture of the Haitian people. It becomes most important to offer our viewers a selection of items that truly can familiarize them with a broad sweep of Haitian history. Recognition, of course, should be given to the Secret Society of Haitian Voodoo. The visual arts of Haiti were transferred from Africa along with religious customs. The visual arts include powerful graphics, sculptures, and masks, deeply incised and painted with bold pigments, body decorations, scarifications, body painting, jewelry, dress, and musical instruments. Voodoo or Vodou, in Haiti and elsewhere in the African Diaspora, now is regarded as a bona fide religion and comes from a highly developed and complex religious tradition. Shown here are several African artifacts used in Haitian Voodoo ceremonies.

ITEMS ON DISPLAY

Scenes from a Voodoo Ceremony/Courtesy Charles L. Blockson Collection/Courtesy The African American Museum in Philadelphia/Vodun or Voodoo was sanctioned as an official religion by the Haitian government. Voodoo represents a considerable portion of the 8.3 million people living in Haiti. These two paintings depict a group of people participating in a Voodoo ceremony.

Shango Staff/20″ x 6″ x 13″/Courtesy Charles L. Blockson Private Collection/Representation of the Ose Shango, priest staff of the Yoruba people of Nigeria, West Africa—a god of lightning and legendary founder of the Yoruba nation.

Gelede Mask/19″ x 11″ x 39″/Courtesy Charles L. Blockson Private Collection/Representing a secret society, this mask was used in various religious ceremonies in Nigeria and other West African countries. Also included are several African masks, fetish figures, and drums.

The Tambour Drum/76″ x 46″/Courtesy Paul and Laura Keene/Standing over six feet high, the Tambour Drum was generally played one time during an important Voodoo ceremony. After the ceremony, the drum was burned. This Tambour Drum represents one of the few drums that are in existence. Paul and Laura Keene received permission in 1952 to bring the drum to Philadelphia from Walter D. Murphy, vice consul of the United States.

GELEDE MASK

THE TAMBOUR DRUM

Paul Jacques Keene Jr./Photograph/Courtesy Paul and Laura Keene/Shown here is the son of Paul and Laura Keene in front of the Tambour Drum. The photograph was taken in 1954 in the garden of Homer Goyne in Petionville, Haiti.

Le Sacrifice du Tambour Assotor/Published in Port-au-Prince, 1943/Courtesy Paul and Laura Keene/Jacques Roumain, one of Haiti's most distinguished men of letters, wrote this rare and important pamphlet describing the importance of the Tambour Drum in secret Voodoo ceremonies.

THE DRUMS

From the distant past until present times, drums are intimately connected to African people. Charged with evocative and mysterious powers, drums are sacred musical instruments. During the violent events that transpired at the tumultuous beginning of the Haitian Revolution, drums played a vital role in helping enslaved Africans to overthrow their masters.

The big drums and the little drums resounded through the night at ten o'clock on August 22, 1791. Legend has it that Boukman, a Jamaican and a Haitian Hougan (or High Priest), on a stormy night on August 15, 1791, at a Voodoo ceremony in the isolated forest of Bois-Caiman near Gros Morne, spoke the following words as he prayed for enslaved Africans to rise against their French slaveowners: "The god who created the sun which gives us light, who rouses the waves and rules the storm, though hidden in the clouds, he watches us. He sees all that the white does. The god of the white man inspires him with crime, but our god calls upon us to do good work."

Boukman ordered his followers to participate in a solemn ritual in which they drank the blood of a slaughtered boar. The night of the revolt, Boukman ordered drums that relayed signals to play until these signals to revolt reached a network of over two hundred drummers. It is reported that six hundred coffee plantations as well as two hundred sugar plantations were set afire by advancing enslaved African people.

The entire northern plain of the island was engulfed in a paroxysm of blood and fire. The Haitian revolt had begun. Boukman was eventually captured by the French and put to death. They put his mutilated body and his decapitated head on a pole as if the very sight of his remains would deter the rest of his Haitian followers. However, instead of terrifying them into subjugation, Boukman's death simply paved the way for the more intense revolt led by his followers Biassou, Toussaint L'Ouverture, Jean-Jacques Dessalines, Henri Christophe, and Jean-Baptiste Chavannes.

ITEM ON DISPLAY

The Conch Shell/8" x 6"/Courtesy Charles L. Blockson Private Collection/Like their African ancestors, Haitians used musical instruments for various reasons such as dancing, funerals, planting and harvesting, initiation rites, and everyday expressions of pleasure and joy. During the Haitian Revolution, drums, gourds, and conch shells were used as forms of communication to alert followers that the Revolution had begun. The coded sounds of the conch shells expressed interpretations that were completely unknown to white people in Saint Dominique. The coded signals played from the conch shells were known as "calling the coumbite." These coded sounds conveyed every hidden signal imaginable: sounds for escaping, hiding, danger, and the call to revolt.

PORTRAIT OF BOUKMAN: INVOKING FREEDOM

THE MAROONS OF HAITI

Enslaved Africans who successfully escaped from slavery and set up free communities in the mountainous interior of Haiti were called Maroons. The Maroons occasionally raided plantations to obtain food and arms among other supplies. The Maroon settlement at La Goyave was made up exclusively of Bosseles, enslaved Africans who had come directly from Africa, called "saltwater blacks."

Shown here is an image of an eighteenth-century Maroon with a conch shell trumpet announcing the revolt of 1791.

ITEM ON DISPLAY

Heroine: Maroon Slave in Action/Oil painting/By Ulrick Jean-Pierre, 1997/18″ x 24″/Courtesy of Picard and Sharon Losier

THE SLAVE REVOLT THAT SHOCKED THE WORLD
A SPARK IN THE DARK

Leading up to the Haitian Revolution, there were numerous violent confrontations between white colonists and enslaved Africans in Saint Dominique. Maroons, runaway slaves who lived in remote areas of the island, constantly raided white-owned plantations for weapons and supplies. François Macandal, the most famous Maroon and *boko* (Voodoo sorcerer), used African traditions and religions to lead a six-year rebellion from 1751 to 1757. He was eventually captured and burned at the stake in Cap-Francais in 1758 by the French authorities.

Boukman Dutty, a Jamaican Voodoo priest, spoke the following words tht sparked the Revolution: "Our god who is good to us orders us to revenge our wrongs. He will direct our arms and aid us. Throw away the symbol of the god of the whites who has so often caused us to weep, and listen to the voice of liberty, which speaks in the hearts of us all."

He swore his followers to loyalty and fidelity. Previously, revolts had taken place, but they were usually short-lived and brutally repressed by the colonial forces. This revolt, however, was seemingly unstoppable, and within six weeks, a thousand whites had been massacred and hundreds of plantations destroyed. One week later, the Haitian Revolution began during the night when hundreds of drums began beating out haunting messages of revolt; spine-tingling pulsations echoed throughout the night—the vibration of Rada tambourines, the tom-tom drums, and the Voodoo drums of Haiti. Boukman was captured and executed. In December 1791, Jean François and Biassou, two of the revolt leaders in an extraordinary act of treachery, offered to surrender the rebel slaves to the French civil commissioner in exchange for the rebel leadership. This opened the way for a man whose name has become almost synonymous with the Haitian Revolution, Toussaint L'Ouverture. Toussaint, a self-educated, middle-aged, former enslaved African, began organizing a disciplined band of rebels, skilled in the art of guerilla warfare. During the next two years, this force won an impressive series of victories over the French armies.

ITEMS ON DISPLAY

Portrait of Boukman: Invoking Freedom/Oil painting/By Ulrick Jean-Pierre, 1997/36″ x 48″/Courtesy of Picard and Sharon Losier

Weapons and Drums: "The Sacred Instruments"/Oil painting/By Ulrick Jean-Pierre, 1997/30″ x 40″/Courtesy of Picard and Sharon Losier

HEROINE: MAROON ENSLAVED WOMAN IN ACTION

WEAPONS AND DRUMS

TOUSSAINT L'OUVERTURE (1743–1803)

Born on May 20, 1743, in a slave hut on the plantation of Count de Breda at Haut De Cap, Haitian patriot and martyr, François Dominique Toussaint L'Ouverture was born with the civil status of an ox. For the next forty-eight years, he remained enslaved, almost untaught. Highborn masters, some descendants of kings, trained in the best universities of France, became part of his retinue. While tending cattle, Toussaint read and educated himself as much as he could. Rising even higher in esteem, he was made overseer of all the enslaved African people on his master's estate. In this post, he was so humble, devout, and eager to please that in time he was held up as a model for all enslaved Africans on the island. This exterior was a mask. Toussaint had an iron determination that one day all, including his master, would be taking orders from him. During this period, he married and raised several children. In less than six years after that, he rose to become the president of the island of Haiti, establishing a record for political and military ability that has rarely been excelled.

When the Haitian slave revolt began in 1791, he was nearly fifty years old. Toussaint joined the rebellion to liberate enslaved Africans and was an organizational genius. Even though Toussaint helped engineer the revolts, he was not in favor of killing helpless women and children. A modest and patient man, he accepted the minor title that Biassou, one of his black leaders, conferred on him, "Doctor in the armies of Kings."

ITEMS ON DISPLAY

Toussaint L'Ouverture Chef des Noirs Ivsurge's des Saint Dominique/Hand-colored print/Courtesy Charles L. Blockson Private Collection/Toussaint sitting upon his horse with a sword in hand.

De Lamartine's Toussaint L'Ouverture/Courtesy Charles L. Blockson Private Collection/Published in Paris, France, in 1857, written by Alphonse de Lamartine, this play is an early celebration of Toussaint L'Ouverture described

TOUSSAINT L'OUVERTURE SIGNS THE CONSTITUTION OF HAITI

as "a cry of humanity in five acts and verse." Slave revolts in the Caribbean were never to be forgotten. They were recorded in imaginative literature, first notably in Henrich Von Kleist's disturbing novella, *Die Verlbung in Saint Dominique*, in 1808. Saint Dominique provided the setting for Victor Hugo's early novel, *Bug Jargal*, the account of a black general based on the life of Henri Christophe. English poet William Wordsworth wrote a sonnet after Toussaint's arrest and imprisonment, while the lengthier work by New England poet John Greenleaf Whittier reflects Toussaint's appeal to abolitionists. Harriet Martineau wrote a three-volume novel on L'Ouverture, the internationally known Haitian leader.

11 Nov A Enseigne Le Grand Destin de Notre Patrie/Courtesy Charles L. Blockson Private Collection/According to tradition, he was a descendant of an African prince named Giaou (Guinow). He married a woman of African descent named Suzanne Simon and adopted her son, a mulatto name Placide. His wife bore him a son named Isaac, who was black like Toussaint. When he passed forty years old, Toussaint had a burning desire to educate himself. He studied with his god-

ABOLITIONIST WENDELL PHILLIPS

father, Pierre Baptiste, an elderly black man. After learning to read and write, Toussaint became an assiduous reader, was christened, and remained loyal to his religion throughout his life.

As virtual master of the island, Toussaint L'Ouverture decided to send all the white officials to France. He also sent Julien Raymond, a mulatto, to France as a commissioner representing Haiti. Attracting international recognition as a military genius, Toussaint became known as the "Black Napoleon." He became a victim of the rising despotism of Napoleon, who could not pardon a black man for having elevated thoughts and having dared to do what he had done himself.

On display are gathered items that are associated with the life and times of Toussaint L'Ouverture: Mahogany bust of Toussaint L'Ouverture/A letter signed by Toussaint/*The Life and Military Achievements of Toussaint L'Ouverture, Late General in Chief of the Armies of St. Domingo*, [Philadelphia]: Printed for the Author (by Henry Sweitzer), 1804/Toussaint L'Ouverture 11 Nous a Enseigné Le Grand Destin de Notre Patrie/The Life of Toussaint L'Ouverture: The Negro Patriot of Haiti/Toussaint L'Ouverture Chef des Noirs Isurgés de Saint Dominique/Toussaint L'Ouverture: An Address Delivered in New York by Wendell Phillips, March 11, 1861/Observations Seru L'Origine Et Les Progrés du Pre Judge Des Colons Blanc Contre Lies Hommes De Couleur, Julien Raymond, Paris, France, January 26, 1791/*Toussaint L'Ouverture Le Napoleon Noir* (Black Napoleon), written by Raphael Tardon, Paris, France, 1951/*The Life of Toussaint L'Ouverture: The Negro Patriot of Hayti*, written by the Reverend John R. Beard, London, 1853.

HAITI'S BLACK TRIUMVIRATE: TOUSSAINT L'OUVERTURE, JEAN-JACQUES DESSALINES, AND HENRI CHRISTOPHE

During those tumultuous days two hundred years ago, violent events transpired in Haiti. It was the time when Napoleon sent his ill-fated expedition to Haiti, intending to make his sister Pauline queen of the island and his brother-in-law, General Charles Victor Emmanuel Leclerc, its ruler. But three former enslaved Africans stood in his way: Toussaint L'Ouverture, Jean-Jacques Dessalines, and

Henri Christophe. Toussaint L'Ouverture, a military genius, ruled Haiti before his betrayal by the French, who tricked him and transported him to France where he died in a French dungeon. Jean-Jacques Dessalines was a ferocious leader, who sprang from a mud and wattle hut in a Guinea swamp. Henri Christophe, surrounded with splendor and pomp as the king of Haiti, was urged on by passion and ambition. These three Haitian generals struggled with their own people as well as their French oppressors to create the first independent black nation in the Americas.

ITEMS ON DISPLAY

Monthly Supplement of the *Penny Magazine of the Society for the Diffusion of Useful Knowledge*, February 28–March 31, 1838/Courtesy Charles L. Blockson Private Collection/This rare newspaper, published in London, provided its readers with a brief but interesting account of L'Ouverture's life.

Monsieur Toussaint projects the tragic destiny of L'Ouverture, the charismatic leader of the first successful slave revolt in the Western Hemisphere that led to the independence of Haiti/Courtesy Charles L. Blockson Afro-American Collection, Temple University

Mahogany bust of Jean-Jacques Dessalines, 21″ x 18″ x 40″/A letter dated December 27, 1805, signed by Dessalines in the second year of Haitian independence and his reign/*Dessalines—A Dramatic Tale: A Single Chapter from Haiti's History*, by William E. Easton, 1892.

JEAN-JACQUES DESSALINES (1758–1806)

On November 18, 1803, nation-founder, emperor, and father of independence, Jacques Dessalines defeated the army of Napoleon Bonaparte in the Battle of Vertieres. Dessalines was born in northern Saint Dominique in 1758 in the hills near the town of Grande Riviere du Nord. Little is known about his natural parents; he was first called Jacques Duclos, taking the name of his cruel owner, who whipped Dessalines repeatedly because of his indomitable spirit. The scars from the whip remained on his body throughout his life and served as a reminder of the terror experienced by enslaved Africans during their enslavement. His only known relative was an aunt named Victoria Montou, called Toya, who fought against the French in the Cahos Mountains during the Revolution. He was sold around the age of thirty to a black freeman and slaveowner and changed his name to this man's last name: Dessalines. Dark-skinned, short in stature, and illiterate, he joined the revolt led by Toussaint L'Ouverture, who made him a general because Dessalines fought with great courage, blind obedience, and great successes in many battles. Dessalines proclaimed the colony independent on January 1, 1804. That same year on September 2, he crowned himself Emperor Jacques I, a few months after Napoleon had proclaimed himself emperor of France. When Dessalines was proclaimed emperor of Haiti, he was addressed as "Majesty," and his wife was called "Empress." He also decreed that all "Negroes" be classified as black, wiping out color distinction. Because of his oppressive rule, on October 17, 1806, while out inspecting his troops at Pont-Rouge, Dessalines was assassinated by mulatto soldiers in his army, who had grown to hate him. Only one mourner, Defilee, a black Haitian woman, sat on the ground beside him weeping until soldiers came to take him to the city cemetery in Port-au-Prince and bury him without a monument. For a long time after, Defilee went every day to scatter wildflowers on the grave of her brave leader who had won Haiti its independence. A monument honoring Jean-Jacques Dessalines stands today in Port-au-Prince.

ITEMS ON DISPLAY

The Flag of Haiti/26″ x 42″/Courtesy Charles L. Blockson Private Collection/The Haitian flag was created when General Jean-Jacques Dessalines, with determination and passion, raised his hands and tore the white out of a French tri-colored flag. Dessalines declared loudly to his army, "Our flag will have no white in it. We will keep

THE FLAG OF HAITI

the blue for the sea that surrounds and defends us, and I want the red for the blood of blacks and mulattos who have liberated our country. Haiti is our country's new name." Private merchants of Philadelphia presented him with a crown brought on the American ship, *The Connecticut*. His coronation robes came from Jamaica, and six white horse-drawn carriages transported Emperor Dessalines and his wife, the Empress Marie-Jeanne, to Le Cap, the site of his coronation.

Creation of the Haitian Flag/Giglee Reproductiono by Ulrick Jean-Pierre, 1980/30" x 40"/Courtesy of Ulrick Jean-Pierre/On May 18, 1803, Jean-Jacques Dessalines, Commander in Chief of the Revolutionary Army, tore the white from the French flag, symbolically acting out the desire to remove the white French colonists from St. Dominique. Dessalines also replaced the flag's initials, "R.F." (for "Republique Francaise") with the words, "Liberte ou la Mort" (Liberty or Death).

Henri Christophe (1767–1820)/Born on the island of Grenada, Henri Christophe, at the age of twelve, was sent to America where he fought in the Revolutionary War in 1789 against the British during the Battle of Savannah, Georgia. He settled in Saint Dominique where he joined black revolutionaries in 1790. A soldier, Christophe was Toussaint L'Ouverture's best general in the Haitian rebellion against the French. After the assassination of Dessalines in 1806, Christophe became president of Haiti from 1807 to 1811. He crowned himself Henri I and served as king of Haiti from 1811 to 1820. He established an aristocracy and created a court as pompous and lavish as those in Europe. He also established schools and improved the economy in Haiti. Christophe strolled about the streets; he carried a stout silver-knobbed cane, dressed in imitation of his model monarch, King George III of England, in a severely plain jacket with no decorations other than a gold star of the Order of Saint.

The Gourd/13" x 8" x 26"/Courtesy Charles L. Blockson Private Collection/"Gourd" is the name of an ornamental trailing or climbing plant. It grows wild in America, Africa, and the Pacific Islands. In Africa, large gourd fruits are dried and used to hold water and other liquids. When Henri Christophe became king of Haiti after Emperor Jean-Jacques Dessalines' violent death, Haiti was bankrupt. Christophe issued an arbitrary act that declared every green gourd in Northern Haiti property of the state. Soldiers were sent to every community to collect them. Before long, 227,000 gourds and calabashes were deposited in the "treasury." Christophe put a value of twenty sous on each; he created the Haitian currency system. Before that year was over, Haiti had metal currency of absolute stability in circulation. Throughout the years, the standard coin of Haiti has been called the gourde.

Sans Souci/Courtesy Charles L. Blockson Private Collection/Located in the village of Milot are remains of King Henri Christophe's palace, Sans Souci, built by French architects. This monument was one of the first edifices

MULATTO ENGINEER, HENRI BARRE, WITH KING HENRI CHRISTOPHE

built by former enslaved Africans who won freedom after the Haitian Revolution. In August 1811, work began on Christophe's palace of Sans Souci, and in September 1812, it was completed. The palace projected four stories above the highest terrace and was built of bricks plastered over with yellow stucco. The roof was of red tile. A grand stairway, flanked at intervals by square stone sentry boxes, led to an exceptionally large open terrace at the western end of the palace. There were banquet halls, an audience chamber, the private rooms of the king and queen, the young prince, Royal, and Christophe's two daughters, the Princesses Amethiste and Athenaire, and quarters for their servants.

Constructed nearby was an arsenal, a royal chapel, a presbytery, special barracks for the palace guards, a storehouse, an equipped printing shop, a stable, offices, and formal gardens. The rooms were paved with marble, paneled with polished hardwoods, and decorated with paintings, tapestries, many mirrors, furniture, and a fine library. The first art academy in Haiti was established in this palace. A specially uniformed black regiment, called the Royal Dahomeys, was installed in the barracks. Christophe's contemporaries proudly stated that Sans Souci rivaled the famous French palace Versailles.

ITEMS ON DISPLAY

The Citadel/Courtesy Charles L. Blockson Afro-American Collection, Temple University/The Citadel La Ferriere, a gigantic fortress that overlooked the Atlantic Ocean, was built by King Henri Christophe to protect his kingdom against the possible return of Napoleon's armies. It is one of the wonders of the modern world. Work on the gigantic fortress began in January 1804 on the orders of Emperor Jean-Jacques Dessalines. A Haitian mulatto engineer named Henri Barre had evolved the design under Christophe's supervision. The fortress took fifteen years to construct; Christophe had been king for seven years before the Citadel was completed. The fortress was at the end of a strenuous three-hour climb up a winding and dangerous trail.

Christophe built it to quarter thirty thousand soldiers. The immense stone structure, consisting of thirty-foot-thick walls, is one hundred thirty feet high. There were dungeons, treasure troves, quarters for nobles and their families, and storerooms that held a supply of food to feed ten thousand men. Some scholars believe that twenty thousand men died in the building of this fortress. The Citadel is a monument that became Christophe's tomb. According to legend, with a silver bullet that he himself hand-mounded years before, Christophe took his own life in 1820.

CANNON IN THE CITADEL

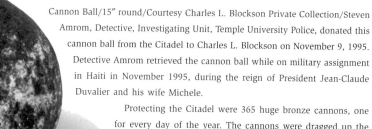

Cannon Ball/15" round/Courtesy Charles L. Blockson Private Collection/Steven Amrom, Detective, Investigating Unit, Temple University Police, donated this cannon ball from the Citadel to Charles L. Blockson on November 9, 1995. Detective Amrom retrieved the cannon ball while on military assignment in Haiti in November 1995, during the reign of President Jean-Claude Duvalier and his wife Michele.

Protecting the Citadel were 365 huge bronze cannons, one for every day of the year. The cannons were dragged up the steep mountainside and ranked in batteries. Hundreds of casks of gunpowder, thousands of fifty-six-, thirty-, and twelve-pound iron cannon balls were borne up the mountain, trailed by panting, sweating men, women, horses, and mules, and piled in chambers behind the cannons, but they were never fired at an enemy.

CANNON BALL

While Detective Steven Amrom was on duty in Haiti, President William J. Clinton sent former United States congressman William H. Gray III of Pennsylvania as a special envoy to Haiti. A few months later, President Clinton sent former president Jimmy Carter, General Colin L. Powell, and Senator Sam Nunn of Georgia to Haiti to negotiate with the government, finally reaching a peace accord with Haiti's military leaders.

Power corrupted Christophe, and excesses marked the years of his reign. In 1820, Christophe committed suicide. He is buried within the Citadel in an unmarked grave. Shown here are a number of items related to Henri Christophe, "Black Majesty of Haiti."

Mahogany bust of Henri Christophe, 15" x 9" x 25"/Letter signed by King Christophe, 1812/Facsimile copy of a royal almanac, 1814, issued at Cap Henri for Emperor Henri Christophe/Letter from Madame Marie Louise Coidavid Christophe, Queen of Haiti, October 7, 1822/*A Mes Concitovens*—A pamphlet by Baron de Vastey, Christophe's secretary, dated January 1815/*Henri Christophe and Thomas Clarkson—A Correspondence*, edited by Earl L. Griggs, 1952/*Black Majesty: "The Life of Christophe, King of Haiti,"* by John W. Vandercook, 1928.

Almanach Royal D'Hayti, Pour L'Annee 1815, Douzieme De L'Independence, Et La Quatrieme Du Regne Desa Majeste Cap Henri [Haiti], 1814/Facsimile cover/Courtesy Charles L. Blockson Private Collection/The original 119-page imperial almanac was issued for Emperor Henry Christophe as an early imprint of Haiti, where printing began in 1789. This is actually far more than an almanac, amounting to a gazetteer of the entire civil list and army, the imperial household, and the emperor's many creations of nobility. Caribbean imprints of the early period are quite rare.

A Mes Concitoyens, Baron de Vastey Cap Henri, Haiti 1815/Courtesy Charles L. Blockson Afro-American Collection, Temple University/Pompee Valentin Baron de Vastey wrote this extremely rare pamphlet, deteriorated through age and use. He was the son of a white man, whose memory he scorned, and a mulatto mother. In the annals of Haitian history, L'Ouverture, Dessalines, and Christophe are heroes; Vastey is almost unknown. He was a highly literate man who served as King Henri Christophe's secretary and as a member of Christophe's Privy Council. Published in 1815 at Cap Henri in the royal printing shop, this twenty-four-page pamphlet is an appeal for black unity when Christophe and Alexandre Sabes Petion controlled the island.

THE FRENCH PRESENCE: NAPOLEON
THE FRENCH REVOLUTION AND THE ERA OF NAPOLEON BONAPARTE

The storming of the Bastille in July 1789 was the first stage in a process that swept away the monarchy, class-based privilege, and sacred institutions. Later, the Revolution would devour its own people and finally end with Napoleon's attempt to enslave Europe and France's colonies in the West

Indies, including Haiti. The equality promised by the French Revolution encouraged the mulattos and blacks of Saint Dominique to seek the same for themselves. Whites on the island had so vigorously opposed a decree granting civil rights to mulattos that it was revoked. In August 1791, a slave revolt broke out in answer to the revocation. The torturing and execution of Vincent Oge, a mulatto spokesperson, who had attended the convention in Paris, provoked atrocities in reprisal. When Napoleon Bonaparte gained power in France, he sent his favorite sister Pauline's husband, General Charles Leclerc, with an expedition of eighty ships and 35,000 men to re-enslave the revolting Haitians in December 1801. When they reached Martinique, the former Caribbean residence of Napoleon's first wife, Josephine, whose mother owned a plantation at Leogane in Saint Dominique, a revolt by enslaved men and women broke out there, also. In Guadeloupe, Napoleon intended to make his sister Pauline queen of Saint Dominique, but Toussaint L'Ouverture stood in his way. Toussaint was later arrested through treachery and taken as a prisoner to France. Angered by Napoleon's treacherous treatment of Toussaint L'Ouverture, Dessalines and Christophe continued the Revolution. Napoleon, while imprisoned on St. Helena Island, later stated, "It was one of my greatest follies; I should not have sent an army to Haiti. I should have contented myself with governing through Toussaint L'Ouverture." Included on display are images of Napoleon, his wife Josephine, his sister Pauline, her husband General Leclerc, Toussaint L'Ouverture, and other items related to the topic.

ITEMS ON DISPLAY

Napoleon Bonaparte/Courtesy Charles L. Blockson Afro-American Collection, Temple University/Military genius, opportunist, tyrant, and demigod—millions of words have been written about Napoleon Bonaparte. He was the man who sent a large portion of his victorious army to recapture Saint Dominique under the leadership of his brother-in-law, General Charles Victor Emmanuel Leclerc.One by one, Toussaint's Generals Dessalines, Christophe, and Maurepas surrendered to Leclerc. Toussaint was later arrested through treachery. Upon embarking, he declared, "with my overthrow, one has merely cut down the trunk of the tree of black freedom, but it will grow from its roots that are numerous and deep."

Napoleon's agents excessively harassed Toussaint during his nine-month imprisonment in the French Alps. He died in his cold dungeon and is buried in an unmarked grave.

Josephine Marie Josèph Rose Tascher Beauharnais (1763–1814)/Courtesy Charles L.

NAPOLEON BONAPARTE

Blockson Private Collection/Napoleon Bonaparte's first wife, Josephine, was born of Creole parents on the French island Martinique. In 1640, during the reign of Louis XIII in France, enslaved Africans were brought to Martinique for the first time. Josephine (known as Rose) was raised on the family sugar plantation near Trois

MARIE JOSÈPH ROSE TASCHER BEAUHARNAIS

Islets. Upon evacuation by the British, Josephine wrote to Toussaint about the plantation, which was in ruins. A correspondence began, and Toussaint repaired and restored the plantation at the expense of the colony and sent the revenues to Madame Bonaparte. Josephine befriended Toussaint's two sons, and they often dined with her at her house.

General Charles Victor Emmanuel Leclerc (1772–1802)/Charles L. Blockson Private Collection/French General Charles Victor Emmanuel Leclerc, husband of Napoleon's favorite sister Pauline Bonaparte, was sent to Saint Dominique by Napoleon, with secret instructions to dispose of the "gilded African," Toussaint L'Ouverture. Upon arrival, Leclerc and General Donatien Rochambeau acquired bloodhounds from Cuba and trained them to attack and mangle Haitian freedom fighters. Leclerc's and Rochambeau's brutal and inhumane terrorism included burying enslaved Africans in the ground with only the heads exposed. Soldiers would decapitate the heads of those buried for amusement. Once Toussaint was betrayed and captured by General Leclerc, he was deported to a prison in France. Shortly after Toussaint L'Ouverture was taken to a dungeon at Fort de Joux in the Jura Mountains area near the Alps, Leclerc died of yellow fever during a sweltering summer in Saint Dominique.

Pauline Bonaparte (1780–1825)/Courtesy of Charles Blockson Private Collection/Of all his siblings, Pauline was Napoleon's favorite. Napoleon intended to make his sister Pauline queen of Saint Dominique. Pauline returned to France after her husband's death.

General de Division and Ancienne Infaterie Francaise/Lithograph prints, hand-colored/Courtesy Charles L. Blockson Private Collection/The first print shows a French general splendidly attired with several ribbons and medals awarded for bravery. The second print shows two infantry soldiers holding a French flag. The uniforms represent the type of clothing worn during Napoleon's campaign when he invaded Saint Dominique.

PAULINE BONAPARTE

HAITI'S FIGHT FOR INDEPENDENCE AT HOME AND ABROAD

From the earliest battles at Lexington and Concord, Massachusetts, in the spring of 1776, to the proclamation of victory at Yorktown, Virginia, eight years later, more than five thousand African American patriots, both enslaved and free, fought in the American Revolutionary War for American independence. Americans were forced to examine the contradictions between ideas of freedom and liberty and the existence of slavery as a violation of natural rights.

Although Africans made significant contributions to the American fight for independence, their participation during the war is often silenced. How many American textbooks tell the story of the all-black regiment from Haiti who fought the bloody Battle of Savannah, Georgia, in 1779? Among the Haitians was Henri Christophe, the twelve-year-old future king of Haiti as well as other valiant colored volunteers who fought for American independence, young men destined to become famous in the Haitian Revolution: the volunteer Chasseurs or the Fontages Legion, named after its French commander. They included Andre Rigaud, Louis Jacques Beavis, Jean Baptiste Mars Belley, who was a deputy to the Paris Convention in 1793, and Martial Besse. The Black Brigade of Saint Dominique, stationed as a rear guard, prevented the annihilation of the allied forces by the British. Christophe fought valiantly and returned to Saint Dominique with slight wounds.

Napoleon had twelve generals and other superior military officers of African descent who served in France and Haiti. General Alexander Dumas, father of the great French novelist Alexandre Dumas, Magloire Pelage, A. Chanalatte, Barthelmy Villate, Etienne V. Mentor, B. Leville, Antoine Clousallate, and Alexandre Petion, future president of Haiti, are the names of some of the generals. Included among the superior officers was Joseph Boulogne, born in Guadeloupe, who, in France, was called Chevalier De St. George, a phenomenal swordsman, dancer, athlete, poet, pianist, and composer. He was sent to Haiti by the French government during the Haitian Revolution.

ETIENNE V. MENTOR

There is an ironic sequel nearly two hundred years later. The descendents of these courageous black volunteers who fought during America's war for independence—known as Haiti's so-called "boat people"—are regularly denied safe entrance into the United States.

ITEMS ON DISPLAY

General Thomas-Alexander Dumas (1762–1807)/Courtesy Charles L. Blockson Private Collection/General Thomas-Alexander Dumas was the son of a wealthy French father, the Marquis Alexandre Antoine Davy de la Pailleterie, and a Haitian mother of African descent, Marie-Cesette. He was a tall and powerfully built man who was fierce in battle. He was a close friend of Napoleon Bonaparte and served under him. When General Dumas questioned Napoleon's motive for invading Egypt, their friendship came to an end. In revenge, Napoleon cut off Dumas's pension and denied him back pay while a prisoner of war. His son Alexandre Dumas, the novelist, could not do justice to the heroic exploits of his incredible father, which are deposited in the French military archives.

GENERAL THOMAS-ALEXANDER DUMAS

Alexandre Dumas, pere (1802–1870)/Courtesy Charles L. Blockson Private Collection/Alexandre Dumas, a literary genius of African ancestry, was the grandson of a Haitian enslaved African woman. His mulatto father became a legendary general in the French Army by the age of thirty-one. Dumas produced an enormous amount of novels and plays that dominated French literature throughout the nineteenth century. Dumas is internationally renowned as the author of *The Three Musketeers* and *The Count of Monte Cristo.*

Alexandre Dumas, fils (1824–1895)/Courtesy Charles L. Blockson Private Collection/Alexandre Dumas, fils, the last of the great Dumas family and son of Alexandre Dumas, was one of the foremost French dramatists of the nineteenth century. His most famous work, *Camille,* performed as a play, became his most popu-

ALEXANDRE DUMAS, FILS, PLAYWRIGHT

ALEXANDRE DUMAS, PERE, NOVELIST

lar work. Success was instantaneous and lasting. Dumas was awarded many literary honors and was elected president of the Academy of Arts. A monument in Paris stands near those of his father, the novelist, and grandfather, the general.

Joseph Boulogne, Chevalier de Saint-Georges (1745–1799)/Courtesy Charles L. Blockson Private Collection/An excellent violinist, renowned conductor and composer Joseph Boulogne, called Chevalier de Saint-Georges, was born in Guadeloupe on December 25, 1745. His mother was an enslaved African of extraordinary beauty named Nanon. She was kidnapped from her home in West Africa when she was a young girl. Because his mother was African, Joseph could not inherit his father's status as a member of the nobility, "Chevalier" meaning "knight." His father, Marquis Jean de Boulogne, governor of the island, was a wealthy white man and owner of the plantation where Joseph spent his early life. At the age of ten, Saint-Georges was sent to France. In Paris, he became a dancer, violinist, poet, swimmer, horseman, composer, and an actor. He was also a phenomenal swordsman. Saint-Georges was arguably the first black composer of classical music, becoming the conductor of Le Concert des Amateur. He became the first person of African descent to join a Masonic Lodge in France. Saint-Georges began his military career in 1761 as an officer in the King's Guard and in 1789 joined the pro-Revolution National Guard, promoted to captain in 1790. In 1792, he became colonel of the Legion des Hussards Americains, comprised of one thousand volunteers of color. In 1795, he took part in the Haitian Revolution. In May 1796, Saint-Georges, with 70,000 muskets, re-armed the troops of Haiti and enabled them to fight more effectively against the British.

Commemorating Patriots of African American Descent at Valley Forge/Print by Cal Massey/12″ x 28″/Courtesy Charles L. Blockson Private Collection/This colorful print depicts the images of three patriots of African descent. More than two thousand African American soldiers were present at General George Washington's winter encampment in 1777–1778 at Valley Forge, Pennsylvania. There were several all-black regiments in the Continental Army including the "Bucks of America," a Massachusetts regiment, who rendered such valuable services that the United States government gave them a special flag. Crispus Attucks, a former enslaved man, was the first person to give his life for American independence during the Boston Massacre on March 5, 1770. In doing so, he sparked the American Revolution. Though few American textbooks tell the story of the all-black regiment from Saint Dominique who fought the bloody Battle of Savannah, Georgia, African American women of the Valley Forge Chapter of Delta Sigma Theta Sorority erected a monument in June 1993 in honor of these gallant men of color. Phillip Sumpter, an African American sculptor, created the stone monument standing nine feet, six inches tall and six feet wide with images from Cal Massey's original painting.

DECLARATION OF INDEPENDENCE IN AMERICA, FRANCE, AND HAITI

The Declaration of America's Independence from Great Britain was signed on July 4, 1776, in Philadelphia, Pennsylvania, our nation's first capital. The Declaration of Independence has been one of the greatest factors in the nation's heritage. Everything stems from it: the Revolution itself, the Articles of Confederation, the Constitution, and the Bill of Rights. Its philosophy and phrases influenced political movements in other countries, particularly the French Revolution.

Benjamin Franklin, while representing the American government in Paris, was instrumental in persuading the French government to send 1,500 men from Saint Dominique to the immediate assistance of the American mainland. Congress sent Franklin to France during the Revolutionary War. Franklin made a deep impression on the French. The alliance he helped form brought France into the war on the side of the hard-pressed Americans. Of Comte d'Estaing, a French admiral of a squadron of the French Navy and former governor of Saint Dominique, when his twenty-four ships sailed into the harbor of Cap-Francais, it was reported that he declared, "My best to Benjamin Franklin, who was instrumental persuading the French colony of Saint Dominique to contribute

RICHARD ALLEN

1,500 to go [to the] immediate assistance of the American mainland." Although a slaveowner himself, Franklin joined the Pennsylvania Abolition Society as its president in 1789, and he wrote a powerful attack against slavery.

News of the 1789 French Revolution affected all three segments of Saint Dominique's society: whites, mulattos, and blacks. As the two segments of elite struggled for control, it was the enslaved Africans who took definitive action. But to understand how the Haitian slave revolution affected the minds and actions of American presidents and statesmen during the era, slavery becomes a critical concern. President George Washington owned a large number of enslaved Africans. In 1793, while Washington was residing in Philadelphia, the Fugitive Slave Act was passed. Washington and members of Congress became involved with legislation. The act provided for the return of runaway slaves to their owners. The Fugitive Slave Law of 1793 strengthened the provisions of the Constitution that protected slavery. It also had a chilling effect on the lives of one-fifth of the American population of African descent. The act prevented Haitian refugees from becoming citizens. When the Haitian Revolution started in 1791, President Washington urged that the United States render every possible aid to France to help "crush the alarming insurrection of the Negroes in Saint Dominique." He implored his friend Thomas Jefferson, also a slaveowner, to offer U.S. aid to the French because of their common vested interests in the institution of slavery. As president, Thomas Jefferson sent Robert Livingston and James Monroe to help in the negotiations with France. In 1803, for about $15 million, 875,000 square miles were added to the area of the United States that became known as the Louisiana Purchase. Napoleon attempted to recapture Haiti, but his armies were defeated in Europe. Needing a vast sum of money, he decided to sell not only New Orleans, but also the whole province owned by France in the United States that reached from the Canadian border to the Americas.

French noble, the Marquis de Lafayette, served General George Washington's forces during the American War for Independence. He saw the birth of America that marked the beginning of a new age in world history. Lafayette declared in a letter to Washington after the war, "I would never have drawn my sword in the cause of America if I could have conceived that thereby I was founding a land of slavery." Because he had participated in the French and American Wars for Independence, he understood the quest for independence by enslaved Haitians. George Washington, whom Lafayette admired as his adopted father, had written that it was "lamentable to see such a spirit of revolution among the black of Saint Dominique."

Alexander Hamilton was the first secretary of the Treasury of the United States. In 1785, Hamilton served as vice president of the New York Society for Promoting Manumission of Slaves and offered enslaved Africans free attorney representation and legal aid. Although Hamilton was an abolitionist, since he was President George Washington's secretary of the Treasury, he agreed to send aid to the white planters of Saint Dominique, largely because Thomas Jefferson and other wealthy southern planters were seething with anger at the black-led revolution in Saint Dominique. In 1804, Hamilton was killed by a pistol shot in a duel with his long-standing political enemy, Aaron Burr.

President John Adams' administration was prepared to accept and even aided Toussaint L'Ouverture's government as long as it was commercially dependent on the United States. There was an incident that appeared in the *Pennsylvania Gazette (Philadelphia)* related to a plot in Philadelphia in 1799 to export "130 French uniform coats, with a large number of linen pantaloons and shirts" to Haiti, which was seized a few doors from the home of Reverend Richard Allen. This was a failed effort to assist Toussaint. However, L'Ouverture sent his assistant Joseph Bunel, a mulatto, and his black wife to Philadelphia where they were invited to dine in the President's House with John Adams and his wife, Abigail. Reportedly, they were the first persons of African descent to dine in a president's house in the United States.

Thomas Paine, born in England, was the most prominent political thinker and writer during the American Revolution who struggled against the British. His influential pamphlet, *Common Sense,* ridiculed the old concept of divine right of kings and called for immediate American independence. He was a genuine lover of liberty and was a member of the Pennsylvania Abolition Society. He was invited to France where he helped draft the French Constitution in 1793. He urged both the French and Americans who had won their independence to recognize the new Republic of Haiti.

Aaron Burr, U.S. senator and the third vice president of the United States, fathered two children, Jean-Pierre Burr and Mary Burr, by Eugenie, a Haitian woman of African descent. Burr also owned land in Haiti and used his Richmond Hill home in New York as a station on the Underground Railroad. His son, Jean-Pierre, who changed his first name to John, played a vital role on the Underground Railroad in Philadelphia. His daughter, Mary Burr, became a well-known seamstress in the city. One of Burr's former mistresses, the daughter of a Philadelphia innkeeper named Lenora Sansay-Nee Hassall, accompanied her husband, a French merchant in Philadelphia, to Saint Dominique. She wrote a book entitled, *Secret History: Or the Horror of St. Domingo, In a Series of Letters, Written by a Lady at Cape Francais to Colonel Burr* in 1808.

GEORGE WASHINGTON

John James Audubon was born in Haiti. His father was an admiral in the French Navy, and his mother was a Creole. He came to Pennsylvania in 1803 where he began to paint birds from life and conducted the first bird-banding experiment in the United States. In 1818, he moved to Kentucky with his wife, and there, Audubon purchased, for the sum of $2,400, two mulatto slaves named William and Lewis Anderson. In 1838, the folio edition of *Birds of America* was completed, and Audubon became known internationally as a painter and ornithologist.

ITEMS ON DISPLAY

George Washington (1732–1799)/Print/Courtesy Charles L. Blockson Afro-American Collection, Temple University/Throughout his life, George Washington and his wife, Martha, owned over three hundred enslaved persons. When enslaved Africans became too difficult to control, he sold them. As president of the United States, Washington brought some of his enslaved persons to Philadelphia even though Pennsylvania outlawed slavery in 1780.

Dr. Benjamin Rush (1745?–1813)/Print/Courtesy Charles L. Blockson Afro-American Collection, Temple University/Born in 1745, Dr. Benjamin Rush was a physician, teacher, and a prominent figure in public life during his times. He was a founding father and signer of the Declaration of Independence as well as a member of the Pennsylvania Abolition Society. Philadelphia's African American leaders, Reverend Richard Allen, Reverend Absalom Jones, and James Forten, considered Dr. Rush to be a respected friend. During the yellow fever plague in 1793, with more than five thousand people dying in Philadelphia, Dr. Rush called upon the African American community to help bury the dead. Many people in the city were convinced that the influx of refugees who poured into Philadelphia to escape from the rebellion that wracked the island of Saint Dominique and other West Indies islands were responsible for the pestilence.

Benjamin Franklin (1706–1790)/Print/Courtesy Charles L. Blockson Afro-American Collection, Temple University/Founding father and a signer of the Declaration of Independence, painter, author, inventor, philosopher, and diplomat, Benjamin Franklin was born in 1706. On the subject of African people, Franklin was at first ambivalent. During a portion of his life, he owned slaves and was openly accused by his political opponents of keeping a black paramour named Barbara. He requested French troops to aid in the American Revolution; among those troops who assisted in the American quest for freedom were eight hundred Haitians.

Thomas Paine (1737–1809)/Print/Courtesy Charles L. Blockson Afro-American Collection, Temple University/Thomas Paine, born in England in 1737, was the most prominent thinker and writer during the American Revolutionary struggle against the British. He is known primarily as the author of *Common Sense*, a pamphlet that set in motion the American quest for independence. Paine was invited to France where he helped draft the French Constitution in 1793. He was a genuine lover of liberty. As a member of the Pennsylvania Abolition Society, Paine bluntly attacked all for slavery and its abuse. He urged both the French and Americans who had won their independence to recognize the new Republic of Haiti.

Thomas Jefferson (1743–1826)/Print/Courtesy Charles L. Blockson Afro-American Collection, Temple University/Thomas Jefferson, a Virginian slaveowner who sired a number of children by Sally Hemings, his enslaved mulatto mistress, was the third president of the United States and the author of the Declaration of Independence. Jefferson considered the black-led Haitian Revolution an act of tyranny and referred to Toussaint L'Ouverture and his followers as "the cannibals of the Republic."

John Adams (1735–1826)/Print/Courtesy Charles L. Blockson Afro-American Collection, Temple University/A signer of the Declaration of Independence and second president of the United States, John Adams was born in Massachusetts in 1735. Both John Adams and his equally famous wife, Abigail, were abolitionists. He once said, "Negro slavery is an evil of colossal magnitude." Even his son, John Quincy Adams, who also became president of the United States, thought slavery was an evil institution.

Alexander Hamilton (1757?–1804)/Print/Courtesy Charles L. Blockson Afro-American Collection, Temple University/Alexander Hamilton was a brilliant statesman who became the first secretary of the Treasury of the United States when he took office in President George Washington's first cabinet. Hamilton was born in Charleston, on the island of Nevis in the British West Indies, in 1757. His father, James Hamilton, was a Scottish merchant, and his mother, Rachel Fawcett, was a Creole of African descent.

Aaron Burr (1756–1836)/Photograph Jean-Pierre Burr, courtesy of Phyllis Morales, descendant of Aaron Burr/Born in 1756, Aaron Burr was a lawyer, a Revolutionary War hero, U.S. senator, and the third vice president of the United States. From 1784 to 1805, he built a brilliant career as a legislator and statesman. Recently, Aaron Burr's descendants, both white and African American, have documented their genealogy as it is connected to Aaron Burr. His descendants reside in Philadelphia and Lancaster County, Pennsylvania, as well as Newark, New Jersey.

Marquis de Lafayette (1757–1834)/Print/Courtesy Charles L. Blockson Afro-American Collection, Temple University/The Marquis de Lafayette, a French nobleman, was a young man who volunteered his services to General George Washington's force during the American Revolutionary War. Lafayette had personally underwritten the American war efforts in the amount of one million dollars. He recognized Haitian rights for independence.

John James Audubon (1785–1851)/Print/Courtesy Charles L. Blockson Afro-American Collection, Temple University/John James Audubon was born in Haiti in 1785. His father was an admiral in the French Navy, and his mother was a Creole from Haiti. She was killed during the slave revolt on the island, and Audubon escaped with his father to France. Audubon was educated in Paris where his artistic talents were developed. The National Audubon Society honors his name.

The American Declaration of Independence/Courtesy Charles L. Blockson Afro-American Collection, Temple University/In 1775, American patriots met in Philadelphia to form the Second Continental Congress. Philadelphia was the seat of the national government from 1775 to 1789. In 1790, it became the national capital again, retaining the distinction until the seat of government moved to Washington, D.C., in 1800. In 1791, when the Haitian Revolution began, many of the signers of the American Declaration of Independence harshly condemned the Haitians' quest for their independence from France.

HAITI'S CONTRIBUTION TO PHILADELPHIA AND BEYOND

French-speaking whites of Saint Dominique were terrified by the prospect of a black-led revolution and possible black rule on the island. Vessels carried hundreds of white refugees (or émigrés), their slaves, and even free people of color from Saint Dominique to Philadelphia, Pennsylvania; Wilmington, Delaware; Baltimore, Maryland; Boston, Massachusetts; Norfolk, Virginia; Charleston, South Carolina; and New Orleans, Louisiana. Many of these refugees sought sanctuary in other colonial islands in the West Indies such as Cuba, Guadeloupe, and Martinique. However, they were forced from these islands fearing that Napoleon would re-institute slavery, which had been abolished during the French Revolution.

Just as Saint Dominique was known as the "Pearl of the Antilles" for its wealth, Philadelphia, the capital of the United States, was called the "Athens of America." Philadelphia's ships and seamen were famous. The city was a community of merchants, mariners, and mechanics. It was urban but pre-industrial with a tree-lined checkerboard of redbrick houses trimmed in white. Philadelphia also had the largest free African American community in America at that time. About six hundred refugees had entered the city in 1792, in spite of Philadelphia's harsh winter weather, because of the determination of the city's anti-slavery leaders who were resolved to enforce Pennsylvania's Gradual Abolition Act of 1780. By this law, guaranteed freedom came to enslaved Africans after six months when any slaveowner established residency in the city. One historian estimates at least 848 refugees of African extraction settled in Philadelphia during this time. Among this group was a number of formerly enslaved African people as well as mulattos who, for the most part, were highly literate and more than reasonably prosperous. They became known in Philadelphia as gens de couleur.

Most of Philadelphia's French-speaking families of color settled in the Society Hill section of the city between Second and Fourth and Race Streets. At first, they experienced language barriers. Before arriving in Philadelphia, many of them were given their freedom by their masters after six months residency in compliance with Pennsylvania's Gradual Emancipation Act. Many brought whatever they could salvage; some came with skills and trades. Most of these gen de couleur families attended St. Mary's, St. Joseph's, or Holy Cross Catholic Churches, where separate segregated pews were provided for them. These churches were all located within walking distance in their expanding French-speaking communities. Those who brought with them a certain

SAMUEL FRAUNCES

amount of wealth and ambition applied their skills as hairdressers, barbers, musicians, tailors, gold-smiths and silversmiths, dressmakers, and house servants to the elite of Philadelphia. Women with coffee-colored complexions from Haiti walked around Head House Square with peanut candy cakes in trays balanced on their heads.

One account states that in Philadelphia there were "Mestizo ladies with complexions of the palest marble, jet black hair, and eyes of the gazelle, and the exquisite symmetry as well as 'coal black' Negress[es] in flowing white dresses and turbans." Frequently, white French gentlemen escorted the women, both dressed richly in West Indian fashion. Writer Moreau de Saint-Mery, a white French native of Saint Dominique, while living in Philadelphia between 1793 and 1798, recorded this observation about these beautiful women of African ancestry claiming that they lived in "the most obnoxious luxury" which can only be provided by the French and by former French colonials.

STEPHEN GIRARD (1750–1831)

Stephen Girard, reported to have been the richest man in America, lived in Philadelphia. Girard was born in Bordeaux, France, in 1750. His father, Pierre, was a wealthy merchant and slave trader in Saint Dominique. Girard settled in Philadelphia in 1776 and owned a bank and other vast financial holdings. His brother John and his attractive black mistress, Hannah, had a daughter named Rosetta, who was born in Haiti in 1772. Girard himself owned enslaved Africans in New Orleans as well as two enslaved young boys in Philadelphia named Abraham and Sam. During the yellow fever plague of 1793, he provided both advice and money to city officials who were combating the terrifying pestilence.

Throughout the years, several historians and scholars wrote that Toussaint L'Ouverture, the Haitian liberator, saved six million francs. After the treacherous capture of L'Ouverture by the French, it was reported that one of Girard's agents in Haiti accepted money from Toussaint, neglecting to return the money back to the Haitian people. One historian, John Bach McMaster wrote, "We see evidence of an allegation that Girard profits from white and Creole Haitians in the 1792 time period." McMaster also describes a September letter to Girard from Haiti's secretary stating that "during the years 1792 and 1793, when the terror of the Revolution covered Cap Haitian with flame, a considerable number of those unfortunate recovered nothing because they had no opportunities to obtain receipts entitling them to withdraw goods from Mr. Girard."

Another view of Girard's wealth pertains to a legal suit entered in Common Pleas Court in Philadelphia in 1886 by Madame Rose de Laulanie of Paris, France, who claimed to be a descendant of L'Ouverture. She demanded restitution of two million dollars. Without documentation, the court denied her case. On display is a hand-

STEPHEN GIRARD

colored lithograph of Girard College. Stephen Girard died in 1831. His controversial will set aside a portion of his estate for Hannah, Girard's housekeeper and his brother John's black mistress. He provided money until her death. He also bequeathed a large sum of money toward the establishment of Girard College on nearly forty acres of land bordering Girard Avenue in North Philadelphia. A stipulation in his will stated that Girard College was for "poor, white, orphan boys only," and that a high stone wall shall be built around it.

This stipulation in his will sparked one of the longest court cases in Philadelphia's legal history. The case, led by Judge Raymond Pace Alexander, was not won until the mid-1960s when Cecil B. Moore, a prominent African American attorney in Philadelphia, along with civil rights leaders like Reverend Martin Luther King and hundreds of others, participated in protest marches at the college. The case was won when the U.S. Supreme Court decided against the legality of Girard's will. Both African American boys and girls attend the school today.

PRESIDENT BOYER'S COTILLION BY F. JOHNSON

HAITIAN REFUGEES' CONTRIBUTIONS TO AMERICA

Although Haitian refugees of African descent were active in many trades in Philadelphia and elsewhere, one of the most long-standing professions was catering. Samuel Fraunces, or "Black Sam" as he was affectionately called even though he was fair-skinned, was born in the West Indies. Recent research reveals that many of his ancestors possessed both European and African bloodlines. Some historians and writers called Fraunces a Haitian Negro. In Haiti and in other Caribbean islands, he would have been known as Affranchis or a mulatto. Keeping with the times, Fraunces wore a white wig after arriving in New York City in 1761. He became one of colonial New York's premier innkeepers. His establishment, known as Fraunces Tavern, still stands today as one of New York's oldest buildings. He served as a patriot during the Revolutionary War, and his tavern became a favorite rendezvous for General George Washington and his staff. After Washington's inaugural in New York as president of the United States, he appointed Fraunces as steward of the executive household. When the nation's capital moved to Philadelphia in 1790, Fraunces became steward in the President's House. He served until 1794 and was known for his culinary skills and as a popular restaurateur. He opened another restaurant in Philadelphia more elegant than his famous Fraunces Tavern in New York City. He is buried in an unmarked grave in St. Peter's Episcopal Church located at Third and Pine Streets, Philadelphia, Pennsylvania.

Peter Augustine, another Haitian refugee of African descent, whose restaurant celebrated the reputation as the "Delmonico of Philadelphia," attracted the families of Philadelphia's white elite and the most distinguished foreign guests, including the Marquis de Lafayette. A plaque in front of his restaurant reads, "Enter: Philadelphia's French Haute Cuisine Gourmet Catering–1815."

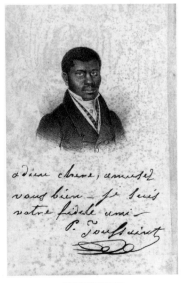

PIERRE TOUSSAINT

PETER ALBERT DUTRIEULLE

St. John Appo, also from Haiti, established his firm at Sixth and Spruce Streets as early as 1804. His Creole wife allegedly had an original recipe for ice cream that was a spécialité de maison. These caterers followed traditions that came directly from Africa, especially in their hot spices, use of salt fish, and the quantities of okra used for thickening. Their sons, William and Joseph Appo, played in Frank Johnson's famous band and orchestra.

Peter Albert Dutrieulle, a descendant of a Haitian family that migrated to Philadelphia in 1793, established a catering business. He was an expert carpenter who made coffins and cabinets. After his death, his family expanded the business with Augustine Baptiste, another Haitian refugee. Descendants of these early Haitian refugee families reside in Philadelphia today along with the Cuyjets, Quad, Abele, Alcindor, Appo, Bartholomew, Dutrieulle, Montiers, Le Count Baptiste, Duterte, and de Roland families.

Born in 1792 in Martinique, Frank Johnson was a major force in American music. With his band and orchestra, he traveled far and wide, building a reputation as a fiddler, bugler, and orchestra leader. In 1824, he wrote a cotillion and a march especially for Haiti's President Nicholas Fabre Geffrard, entitled, "Recognition March on the Independence of Haiti," for performance at the Grand Ball at the New Theater in honor of General Marquis de Lafayette. Later, Lafayette sponsored a European tour for Johnson, where he played before Queen Victoria of England. Edward Roland, born in Haiti in 1804, came to Philadelphia and played in Frank Johnson's orchestra.

Haitian refugees also established reputations in New York City and elsewhere in the country. Theodore Duplessis in New York City was known for his superlative ice cream. Pierre Toussaint, born in Haiti in 1776 a slave, came to New York with his owners when they fled from Haiti after the slave revolt. Pierre had been taught to read and write. He apprenticed as a hairstylist. Among his regular customers were Alexander Hamilton's wife and the daughter of the Revolutionary War general Philip Schuyler. When his owner died, his widow offered to give Pierre his freedom. He supported her until her death. She was destitute by poor investments. Pierre became wealthy, bought his freedom and the freedom of several other enslaved Africans, sheltered and trained homeless black boys, and nursed victims of yellow fever while thousands fled the city. He supported orphans, contributed to the building of churches, and raised a large part of the money for the first Catholic orphanages in New York City. He died in 1853 at the age of eighty-seven, outliving both his wife and their adopted daughter, Euphemia. In 1997, Pope John Paul II declared Pierre Toussaint venerable, an important step on the way to possible Catholic sainthood.

Jean Baptiste Point Du Sable was born in San Marc, Haiti, in 1745. His father was a French privateer, and his mother was a Haitian. Du Sable immigrated to the United States and became a fur trapper. He established trading posts on the sites of the present cities of Michigan City, Indiana; Peoria, Illinois; and Port Huron, Michigan. In 1772, Du Sable constructed a log cabin home for his wife and family that is recognized as the first settlement of Chicago, Illinois. Du Sable is known as the "Father of Chicago."

In Wilmington, there were several French-speaking Haitian families who settled in the city after fleeing from Haiti during the slave revolts of 1793 and 1798. John Garesche became a prosperous real estate owner.

ITEMS ON DISPLAY

Stephen Girard/Print/Courtesy Charles L. Blockson Afro-American Collection, Temple University

Girard College/Colored Lithograph/Courtesy Charles L. Blockson Afro-American Collection, Temple University

Samuel Fraunces/Photograph/Courtesy Charles L. Blockson Afro-American Collection, Temple University

Peter Albert Dutrieulle/Photograph/Courtesy Charles L. Blockson Afro-American Collection, Temple University

General Marquis de Lafayette/Photograph/Courtesy Charles L. Blockson Afro-American Collection, Temple University

Frank Johnson/Record Album with Portrait/Courtesy Charles L. Blockson Afro-American Collection, Temple University

Pierre Toussaint/Photograph with wife, Madame Toussaint, and adopted daughter, Euphemia/Courtesy Charles L. Blockson Afro-American Collection, Temple University

Memoir of Pierre Toussaint/Book/Courtesy Charles L. Blockson Afro-American Collection, Temple University

Jean-Baptiste Point Du Sable/Photograph and Calendar/Courtesy Charles L. Blockson Afro-American Collection, Temple University

COLONIZATION AND EMIGRATION WITHIN THE AFRICAN DIASPORA

During the years 1793–1798, hundreds of French-speaking and free persons of color immigrated to Philadelphia and other eastern seaboard cities; men like Thomas Jefferson had thought it feasible to combine gradual emancipation with deportation of African Americans. Shortly after the close of the War of 1812, an African American ship owner, Paul Cuffee of New Bedford, Massachusetts, took thirty-eight African Americans on board the vessel *The Traveler* and sailed for Sierra Leone in West Africa, paying all their expenses out of his own pocket. Captain Cuffee thought they would find a better life in their motherland, away from racial prejudice in America. Cuffee was familiar with the writing of Olaudah Equiano, who was captured as a young boy from Nigeria, West Africa, when he was eleven years old. For thirty years, he sailed the seas with various masters, visiting Saint Dominique and other Caribbean islands. In Philadelphia, a Quaker named Robert King owned him. After he gained his freedom, he settled in England and wrote his autobiography in 1789. His two-volume autobiography helped the British government to abolish slavery in Great Britain.

GENERAL MARQUIS DE LAFAYETTE

Of the various personalities who achieved prominence in Philadelphia, Prince Saunders is one of the least known today. He was born a free African American in Vermont of parents from Haiti. Saunders became one of the renowned black educators, lecturers, and politicians of his day. When visiting Haiti, Saunders became a confidant of King Henri Christophe and taught his children. He introduced the vaccination to the children of Haiti. In 1816, Saunders published the *Haytian Papers*, a translation and commentary of the Code Henri, together with documents concerning the Haitian Revolution. In 1818, Saunders came to Philadelphia and officiated as a lay reader at St. Thomas African Episcopal Church, making the acquaintance of Philadelphia abolitionists. Saunders encouraged African Americans to immigrate to Haiti.

Within a few years of Paul Cuffee's experiment, the American Colonization Society was formed under the leadership of such prominent slaveholders as John C. Calhoun, John Randolph, Bushrod Washington, and Francis Scott Key, who wrote "The Star-Spangled Banner," the national anthem of the United States. They persuaded Congress to purchase territory in West Africa that they named Liberia. At the very outset, free African Americans and white abolitionists attacked the society. In 1817, an audience of three thousand Philadelphians heard the two prominent African American leaders Reverend Richard Allen and James Forten brand the American Colonization Society as an "outrage" formed for the benefit of slaveholding interest. In 1824, during his administration, Jean-Pierre Boyer welcomed free African Americans to Haiti and granted opportunities to cultivate and to labor at their tasks as mechanics. Every facility of the Haitian government was to be offered to them.

That same year, under the leadership of Bishop Allen, a group of people met in Mother Bethel A.M.E. Church and accepted invitations to immigrate to Haiti and later that year sailed for Samana, Haiti, now the Dominican Republic.

The newly arrived immigrants remained together and established the first African Methodist Episcopal Church under the name of St. Peter's and elected Reverend Richard Robinson as pastor. Ships carrying African Americans landed at three places: Santo Domingo, Puerto Plata, and the coast of the Samana Peninsula.

James Forten was born of free parents in 1766. He served as a powder boy during the American Revolutionary War. He later became a wealthy sailmaker. Forten served as one of the managers of the Haitian Emigration Society and gave the plan to immigrate to Haiti his heartfelt

WILLIAM WELLS BROWN

endorsement. John Summerset, Forten's friend and an oysterman, left for Haiti with two of Forten's sailmaking apprentices. James Forten maintained an active interest in Haiti for the rest of his life.

Robert Douglass Jr., the son of Forten's friend Robert Douglass Sr. and Grace Bustill Douglass, was a well-known artist in the 1830s. He spent a year and a half in Haiti and traveled throughout the island painting and meeting prominent people, including Prince Saunders, who had returned to Haiti and ended his days in Port-au-Prince.

WILLIAM WELLS BROWN (1814?–1884)

Born under the cruel system of slavery in Lexington, Kentucky, in 1814, William Wells Brown became another prominent African American who acquired an interest in Haiti. Brown was a renowned anti-slavery orator, a professional man of letters, and a practicing physician. He traveled to Europe in 1849, and while he was there, he wrote and lectured in the highest circles. In the fall of 1855, Brown returned to America. While visiting Philadelphia, he lectured at St. Thomas Episcopal Church on "St. Domingo: Its Revolutions and Its Patriots." Brown's subject was about the violent struggle that led to the creation of Haiti and included a prediction of similar violence in the slaveholding American South. He encouraged immigration to Haiti that same year.

ABRAHAM LINCOLN (1809–1865)

Abraham Lincoln, the sixteenth president of the United States, was a colonizationist at heart. On February 1, 1864, Lincoln made the following order to Edwin M. Stanton, Secretary of War. "You are directed to have a transport (either a steam or sailing vessel, as may be deemed proper by the Quartermaster-General) sent to the colored colony established by the United States at the Island of Vache (or Cow Island), on the coast of San Domingo, to bring back to this country such of the colonists there as desire to return." Of the 431, about 378 returned alive; some were seriously ill. Lincoln's order was a total failure.

ABRAHAM LINCOLN

AFRICAN AMERICANS IN HAITI

The combined effects of the Federal Civil Rights Act of 1866, the Reconstruction Act of 1867, and the ratification of the Fourteenth Amendment in 1868 brought some legal protection to African Americans in the North and in the South. A new day had dawned within the African American community throughout the nation. From 1870 to 1901, African Americans served their states as congressmen; Southern African Americans sat in every Congress from the Forty-first to the Fifty-sixth with one exception. Although half of them were formerly enslaved, the group included brilliant men and superb orators, and several of them were appointed to represent the United States in Haiti.

JOHN MERCER LANGSTON (1829–1897)

John Mercer Langston, born in Virginia in 1829, was a prominent abolitionist, educator, lawyer, and reformer. A relative of Langston Hughes, the celebrated African American poet and writer, John Mercer Langston served two terms as consul general to Haiti. In his autobiography, he wrote of his disillusionment about the economic conditions in Haiti, the recurrent revolution, and the problem of asylum in the residence of diplomats. Langston also served as the West Indies attorney for John Wanamaker and Company of Philadelphia.

EBENEZER DON CARLOS BASSETT

EBENEZER DON CARLOS BASSETT (1833–1908)

Born in Litchfield, Connecticut, in 1833, Ebenezer D. Bassett, a Reconstruction leader, studied at Yale College and the University of Pennsylvania. From 1857 to 1869, Bassett was principal of the Institute for Colored Youths in Philadelphia. In 1869, President Ulysses S. Grant appointed him to the post of minister resident of the United States to Haiti, the first diplomatic appointment of an African American by the federal government. Bassett served as consul general of Haiti from 1879 to 1888. In 1888, the year Bassett returned to the United States, President Benjamin Harrison appointed Frederick Douglass minister resident and consul general of the Republic of Haiti and charge d'affair of the Dominican Republic. Upon returning to the United States in 1892, Bassett published *The Handbook of Haiti.*

FREDERICK DOUGLASS (1817?–1895)

Born in Maryland in 1817, Douglass, a former slave, became a skilled abolitionist, orator, journalist, reformer, and public servant. Douglass was well received by the Haitians, reflecting their awareness of his long career as a reformer. Benjamin Harrison appointed Douglass as minister resident and consul general of the Republic of Haiti and charge d'affair of the Dominican Republic.

JOHN STEPHEN DURHAM

John Stephen Durham succeeded Frederick Douglass as a minister to Haiti. Durham was born in Philadelphia in 1861 and was a lawyer, author, and journalist. He was the son of African American parents, well known in Philadelphia for several generations. His uncles, Clayton and Jeremiah Durham, having been noted clergymen, helped Bishop Richard Allen found the African Methodist Episcopal Church (Mother Bethel). Durham was a graduate of the Institute for Colored Youth. He

FREDERICK DOUGLASS

was fluent in French and Spanish and was appointed as United States Consul General in the Dominican Republic by President Benjamin Harrison. Both Haiti and the Dominican Republic share the same island. In 1902, Durham published *Diane, Priestess of Haiti*. The story first appeared in the April edition of *Lippencott's Monthly Magazine*.

Nearly one hundred years later, Judge Raymond Pace Alexander was sent to Haiti as an advisor, representing the United States government. As young attorneys, Alexander and his equally famous wife, Sadie Tanner Mossell Alexander, challenged Stephen Girard's will, which had established a school for white boys only. The Alexanders paved the way for another prominent Philadelphia attorney, Cecil B. Moore, who with assistance from the Philadelphia branch of the NAACP, won the Girard case in the United States Supreme Court. Through the efforts of Moore and Alexander, Girard College was opened for the first time to African American youngsters.

Former United States representative Reverend William H. Gray III traveled to Haiti on several occasions, providing the country with food, medical supplies, and other necessary life-supporting commodities. Former four-star general in the United States Army, national security advisor, and present secretary of state, Colin Powell was sent to Haiti on a series of peace missions by Presidents Bill Clinton and George W. Bush after political upheaval within the Haitian government.

ITEMS ON DISPLAY

Olaudah Equiano/Print/Courtesy Charles L. Blockson Afro-American Collection, Temple University

Prince Saunders/Photograph of Book/*Haitian Papers, A Collection of the Very Interesting Proclamation and Other Documents of the Kingdom of Haiti*, London, 1818/Courtesy Charles L. Blockson Afro-American Collection, Temple University

PRINCE SAUNDERS

REVEREND ABSALOM JONES

Reverend Absalom Jones/Photograph/Courtesy Charles L. Blockson Afro-American Collection, Temple University

James Forten/Photograph and Certificate of Copyright Book, St. Domingo/Courtesy Charles L. Blockson Afro-American Collection, Temple University

Senator Charles Sumner's Speech *Independence of Haiti and Liberia, April 23 and 24, 1862.* Pamphlet/Courtesy Charles L. Blockson Afro-American Collection, Temple University

President Abraham Lincoln/Photograph/Courtesy Charles L. Blockson Afro-American Collection, Temple University

Pennsylvania Colonization Society Incorporated/Broadside/Courtesy Charles L. Blockson Afro-American Collection, Temple University

A Guide to Haiti/By James Redpath (1861)/Courtesy Charles L. Blockson Afro-American Collection, Temple University

John Mercer Langston/Photograph/Courtesy Charles L. Blockson Afro-American Collection, Temple University

Frederick Douglass/Photograph/Letter (Facsimile) from Frederick Douglass to Ebenezer Bassett, August 25, 1890/Courtesy Charles L. Blockson Afro-American Collection, Temple University

Ebenezer Don Carlos Bassett/Photograph/Courtesy Charles L. Blockson Afro-American Collection, Temple University

John Stephen Durham/Photograph/Book/*Priestess of Haiti*, Philadelphia (1902)/Courtesy Charles L. Blockson Afro-American Collection, Temple University

Judge Raymond Pace Alexander/Photograph/Courtesy Charles L. Blockson Afro-American Collection, Temple University

Attorney Cecil B. Moore/Photograph/Courtesy Charles L. Blockson Afro-American Collection, Temple University

Reverend William H. Gray III/Photograph/Courtesy Charles L. Blockson Afro-American Collection, Temple University

Secretary of State Colin Powell/Photograph/Courtesy Charles L. Blockson Afro-American Collection, Temple University

TWO CENTURIES OF SURVIVAL: AGAINST ALL ODDS

The demise of slavery signaled the birth of hope among Haitians of African descent. The French were defeated at the Battle of Vertieres, resulting in the victorious proclamation of Haitian independence on January 1, 1804, sixty years before slavery was abolished in the United States. In their public and private lives and their cultural and political activities, Haitians confidently turned their energies to what they perceived to be the sizable task of removing the residue of violence, racism, and poverty that remained in the society around them. Jean-Pierre Boyer, who became the president of Southern Haiti in 1818 after Henri Christophe's death, united the country in 1820. Boyer seized the Dominican Republic, which won its independence in a revolution in 1844. For the next seventy years, the country was ruled by a series of dictators.

Beginning in 1844, the predominantly black army installed four heads of African descent in office, in an attempt to reduce the mulattos' influence in government. In 1849, the fourth of these leaders, Faustin Elie Soulouque proclaimed himself Emperor Faustin I. He ruled for ten years in a despotic manner until early 1859 when he was forced out of office by Nicholas Fabre Geffrard, the son of a black father and mulatto mother. Geffrard restored republican government, but he was, in turn, exiled in 1867. The struggle for control of the government continued.

Between 1844 and 1915, there were twenty-two dictators in Haiti, each unable to address the poverty, racism, environmental degradation, violence, and instability that characterized most Haitians' lives.

In 1915, President Guillaume Sam was murdered by an angry mob. President Woodrow Wilson sent United States Marines to protect American interests in Haiti. Franklin Delano Roosevelt, assistant secretary to the Navy under Wilson, was chief author of the Declaration of Haiti in 1914–1915. The president announced to the world that he sent the marines to occupy Haiti because there was turmoil in the country. However, the issue centered on the First National Bank and the Central Bank of Haiti, controlled by the United States, and the Haitian people decided that they did not want a foreign nation controlling the Central Bank of Haiti. This defiant act gave the United States provocation to invade Haiti. The American occupation forces began to treat Haitian citizens harshly, manipulated elections, dissolved the legislation, and indulged in the most flagrant kinds of racism.

Led by Charlemagne Peralte, groups of Haitian freedom fighters, using guerilla warfare tactics, began to attack the marines. Peralte declared his ambition to "drive the Yankee invaders into the sea." He was prepared to make any sacrifice to liberate Haitian territory. Peralte was captured and assassinated by the marines, and more than two thousand Haitians were killed or wounded. As proof of Peralte's death, his body was tied to a door in Grande Riviere du Nord and photographed.

In 1922, President Philippe Sudre Dartiguenave was ousted and replaced by Louis Borno, in the second-ever constitutional transfer of power in Haiti's history. The marines remained in Haiti until 1934, during Roosevelt's term as president. The American government controlled Haiti's finances for several years after the troops left.

In 1937, Haitians sought work in the Dominican Republic sugar estates but were not welcomed. Consequently, approximately ten thousand Haitian immigrants living in the Dominican Republic were rounded up and murdered.

Two years before World War II began, in 1939, President Stenio J. Vincent, first elected in 1930, took steps to remain in office beyond the expiration of his second term. He resigned after strong opposition by the Haitian people and United States' disapproval. Haiti declared war on Germany and Japan in 1941, permitted the United States' anti-submarine aircraft to make use of the Port-au-Prince landing field, and supplied needed products throughout the war. Haiti became a charter member of the United Nations in 1945.

The Haitians adopted a new constitution in 1950 and elected Paul E. Magloire president. Magloire assumed dictatorial powers in December 1956 but was forced to resign a few days later.

ALEXANDRE SABES PETION

LETTER WRITTEN BY PRESIDENT SALOMON

FAUSTIN, EMPEROR OF HAYTI, IN HIS CORONATION ROBES.

ADELINA, EMPRESS OF HAYTI, IN HER CORONATION ROBES.

HIS IMPERIAL MAJESTY FAUSTIN, EMPEROR OF HAYTI.

The political history of St. Domingo, or Hayti, where his royal black and Imperial Majesty Emperor Faustin I. reigns, is a curious chapter in the world's history. Discovered in the fifteenth century, by Columbus, St. Domingo is one of the largest and most fertile of the West India Islands. It is situated between the island of Jamaica and Cuba, and extends in length from east to west nearly 400 miles, and in breadth from 60 to 150 miles. About the middle of the sixteenth century, the island of St. Christophers was taken possession of by a mixed colony of French and English; but,

having excited the jealousy of the Spaniards, they were driven from it. They turned pirates or buccaneers, as they were called, and at last succeeded in making good a footing in St. Domingo itself. By the treaty of Ryswick that part of the island on which they had established themselves was ceded to the King of France, who acknowledged them as his subjects, and gave them his protection. In 1722 the colony was in a very prosperous condition, and continued so till 1789, when the great French Revolution broke out. The population of St. Domingo was divided into three classes—the whites, the people of colour, and the slaves. All the power and influence were concentrated in the whites, who disdained any intercourse with the people of colour. The black slaves ranked still lower,

experiencing great cruelty from the two other classes. When the French national Convention passed the memorable decree that all men were born equal, and entitled, therefore, to an equality of civil privileges, it became the signal for revolution in the island. Whilst the whites and people of colour were at war, the black population suddenly rose in a body and emulated the Figaro Siciliennes by putting to death all the whites who came in their way without distinction of age or sex. Lamartine's hero, Toussaint Louverture, who assumed the command of the insurgents in 1794, was recognised by the French Directory. In May, 1801, Toussaint promulgated a constitution and declared the independence of the island. In

FIRST SALE OF SUGAR IN THE MARKET-SQUARE OF D'URBAN, PORT NATAL.—(SEE NEXT PAGE.)

FAUSTIN ELIE SOULOUQUE AND HIS WIFE ADELINA

After a period of unrest, the army seized control until elections were held in September 1957. It was then that François Duvalier became president. Known as "Papa Doc," Duvalier, a physician, won the respect of the Haitian people by improving the conditions of the poor and by attracting international business to improve Haiti's economy. He later earned the reputation as an oppressive leader; a large number of Haitians were retained in the infamous Fort Dimanche prison.

Because of the oppressive conditions, unknown numbers of Haitians fled the country. Duvalier organized the Tonton Macoutes as his personal police force. They were known for their brutality and corruption and were feared by Haitian citizens. Duvalier encouraged them to participate in Voodoo ceremonies. The Tonton Macoutes trademark was dark-shaded sunglasses. President Duvalier's son Jean-Claude Duvalier, known as "Baby Doc," was elected "president for life" after his father's death. He also employed the Tonton Macoutes to protect him during his oppressive regime. On February 7, 1986, President Jean-Claude and his wife Michele fled from Haiti to France after being forced out by an uprising, ending a twenty-nine-year Duvalier family dictatorship.

The army chief, Lieutenant General Henri Namphy, was named to oversee two years of transition to democracy. On December 16, 1990, after a series of coups, Jean-Bertrand Aristide, a former Catholic priest, was overwhelmingly elected president in Haiti's first free and peaceful voting election. He was sworn in as president on February 7, 1991, and immediately announced reorganization of the army. On September 30, 1991, Aristide was overthrown by the military in a violent coup led by Lieutenant General Raoul Cedras. On October 8, 1991, the military installed Supreme Court Justice Joseph Nérette as provisional president. About two hundred United States troops arrived as part of the United Nations' plan to restore democracy in Haiti on October 11, 1993.

On May 8, 1994, President William J. Clinton announced that the United States would cease returning the "boat people" to Haiti without hearing their claims for refugee status. Fleeing Haitians were permitted to make their claims aboard United States ships in the Caribbean or in other countries. That same month, President Clinton named William H. Gray III, former congressman from Pennsylvania, as special envoy to Haiti. On September 17, Clinton sent former president Jimmy Carter, General Colin L. Powell, and Senator Sam Nunn of Georgia to Haiti to negotiate with Cedras. Aristide returned to Haiti on October 15, 1994, and regained the presidency. He left the priesthood and married.

In January 2004, during Haiti's independence bicentennial celebration, university students and other demonstrators marched against President Aristide in a series of protests demanding Aristide's resignation. Student-led protests and strikes helped to oust President Elie Lescot in 1946, Paul Magloire in 1956, and Jean-Claude Duvalier in 1986. Refusing to resign, President Aristide pressed France for restitution demanding $21.7 billion to cover what Haiti paid for the recognition of its independence two hundred years ago when enslaved Haitians created more wealth for France than any of its other colonies. The restitution claim represents forty-four times Haiti's current annual budget.

PRESIDENTIAL DOCUMENTS SIGNED BY VARIOUS PRESIDENTS AND OTHER HAITIAN OFFICIALS

Alexandre Sabes Petion (1770–1818)/Print and Letter/Courtesy Charles L. Blockson Collection/Born in Port-au-Prince, Alexandre Petion, the quadroon son of a white French artist and a mulatto woman, was a scholar, soldier, and painter. When Christophe gained control of the northern part of the island after the death of Dessalines, Petion as president maintained his power in the south, in what is now the Dominican Republic. Petion opened his ports to all nations and paid all debts. In his communication with the representatives of a foreign power, Petion demonstrated his desire to secure law and order. Petion died in 1818. After Petion's death, Jean-Pierre Boyer succeeded him. Boyer unified the island in 1822 by taking what had been the Spanish half./Courtesy Charles L. Blockson Collection, Temple University/President Sylvain Salnave/President Hyppolite/President Tiresias Augustin Simon

Sam/President Nord Alexis/President François Antoine Simon/President Joseph Davilmar Theodore/President Stenio Vincent/President Dumarsais Estimé/President Paul E. Magloire/President Louis Borno/Photograph/J.G.D. Mario, General De Division Commandant L'Arrondissement des Cayes/President Louis Salomon/President François Duvalier/Mimeographed Document/Signed by the president of Haiti. Nine-page folio, Port-au-Prince, April 11, 1961. Highly detailed orders regarding the constitution with a list of all the arrondissements.

Faustin Elie Soulouque (1785–1867) and his wife Adelina/Courtesy Charles L. Blockson Private Collection/After the presidency of Jean-Pierre Boyer came that of Faustin Elie Soulouque, formerly enslaved African and veteran of Haiti's wars against France. After defeating his mulatto supporters in 1849, he led a scorched-earth invasion of the southern part of the island, now the independent Dominican Republic. Ten years of carnage within Haiti followed until he was overthrown by a revolution led by Nicholas Fabre Geffrard.

Haiti Leaders and Presidents/Pictorial Print/Courtesy Charles L. Blockson Private Collection/This panoramic color print shows images of Haitian leaders and presidents who ruled Haiti during the past two hundred years. The images range from Toussaint L'Ouverture to President Jean-Bertrand Aristide.

Constitution De La Republica D'Haite/Courtesy Charles L. Blockson Private Collection/The United States government imposed this constitution during occupation. Written in the United States as a formality, it was submitted to a plebiscite on June 12, 1918. The constitution was in effect until 1934 when President Franklin Delano Roosevelt withdrew the United States Marines from Haiti. This pamphlet was published in Port-au-Prince in 1918.

The United States Occupation of Haiti, 1915–1934/Courtesy Charles L. Blockson Afro-American Collection, Temple University/President Woodrow Wilson sent the United States Marines to Haiti in 1915 in what was intended as a short-term measure because of the fear that Germany might establish submarine bases there that would threaten American shipping and the Panama Canal. But the Marines remained in Haiti for twenty years, long after the German threat disappeared.

Charlemagne Peralte (1886–1919)/Courtesy Charles L. Blockson Afro-American Collection, Temple University/Shown here is a gruesome photograph of Haitian freedom fighter and hero, Charlemagne Peralte, taken after his assassination by two United States Marines disguised as Haitians in 1919. He resigned from the Haitian Army in 1915 and returned to his home in Hinche to become a farmer. He led a successful guerrilla resistance movement against U.S. occupation. The photograph was circulated in an attempt to undermine anti-American resistance. Official reports put the number of Haitians killed by marines at 3,250 in the first five years of the occupation.

President Franklin Delano Roosevelt (1882–1945)/Courtesy Charles L. Blockson Afro-American Collection, Temple University/The thirty-second president of the United States, 1933–1945. Early in his career as assistant secretary of the Navy under President Woodrow Wilson, Roosevelt was the chief author of the Declaration of Haiti in 1914–1915.

Mémoires d'Un Leader Du Tiers Monde Mes Négociations Avec Le Saint Seige on Une Tranche D'Histoire, 1969/Courtesy Charles L. Blockson Private Collection/This book, published in Haiti, is the memoirs of former president François Duvalier. The book contains photographs of Duvalier's family, administrative staff, and those of foreign dignitaries, as well as letters and other documents pertaining to Duvalier's authoritarian rule in Haiti as "President for Life."

Simone Ovide Duvalier (1913–1997)/Courtesy Charles L. Blockson Private Collection/She married President François Duvalier in 1939 and became known as "Mama Doc." She was a nurse and the daughter of a mulatto merchant in the prosperous suburb of Petionville. She birthed four children: Marie-Denise, Simone, Nicole, and

Jean-Claude. After her husband's death in 1971, she served as de facto ruler of Haiti until 1974. Mrs. Duvalier remained very powerful until her son, Jean-Claude Duvalier, was ousted in 1986.

The Duvaliers "Papa Doc" and "Baby Doc"/Courtesy Charles L. Blockson Private Collection/For almost three decades, Haiti was associated with a ruthless dynastic dictatorship all but synonymous with the names of President François Duvalier and his son, Jean-Claude Duvalier. Their regime did not tolerate opposition. The Duvaliers ruled Haiti with an iron hand using the Tonton Macoutes, their secret police.

SIMONE OVIDE DUVALIER

THE DUVALIERS "PAPA DOC" AND "BABY DOC"

President Jean-Claude Duvalier and his wife, Michele Bennett Duvalier/Photograph/May 27, 1980/Courtesy Charles L. Blockson Afro-American Collection, Temple University/Pictured are "President for Life" Jean-Claude Duvalier and his wife Michele Bennett Duvalier at their wedding in Port-au-Prince Cathedral. Jean-Claude inherited his father François Duvalier's reputation as a dictator who brought unimaginable suffering to the Haitian people. The extravagant wealth of the Duvaliers, the abject poverty of the Haitian people, and the savagery of the Tonton Macoutes were the impressions that formed the world's perception of Haiti. In 1986, there were demonstrations, riots, and finally a revolt against President Jean-Claude Duvalier. With assistance from the United States government, Duvalier and his wife Michele were flown to France on a private airplane. The Duvaliers were divorced, and both currently reside in France.

HAITI LIBERÉ 7 FEVRIER

The Tonton Macoutes/Photograph/Courtesy Charles L. Blockson Afro-American Collection, Temple University/A Tonton Macoute stands on duty in Port-au-Prince before Jean-Claude Duvalier's departure from Haiti. Tonton Macoutes, organized by President François Duvalier as his personal police force, were encouraged by him to participate in Voodoo ceremonies. The Duvaliers employed only dark-skinned Haitians as members of the Tonton Macoutes, whose trademark was dark-shaded sunglasses.

Haiti Liberé 7 Fevrier 1986/Courtesy Charles L. Blockson Private Collection/Most Haitian artists refrained from direct political comments during the regime of President François Duvalier. Copied from the original painting by Haitian artist Edouard Duval-Carrie in 1979,

FLOWER-COVERED HEARSE CARRYING PRESIDENT "PAPA DOC" DUVALIER

this poster is a daring satirical reference to the rumors about President Duvalier's son Jean-Claude's sexual preferences and unstable character. The artist suggests in his painting that Jean-Claude should commit suicide. Duval-Carrie illustrates illusion and metaphor as powerful tools in political art.

Flower-Covered Hearse Carrying President "Papa Doc" Duvalier/Courtesy Charles L. Blockson Private Collection/President François Duvalier died on April 21, 1971. As Duvalier lay in state, crowds filed past his body, which was guarded by twenty-two soldiers and twenty Tonton Macoutes. When the funeral took place on Saturday, April 24, every church bell in Port-au-Prince tolled and a 101-gun salute boomed out over the city.

ITEMS ON DISPLAY

21 Postcards and 5 Photographs of Haiti/1920s (two inscriptions are dated 1922)/From 9 cm to 15 cm/Courtesy Charles L. Blockson Afro-American Collection, Temple University/Illustrations of various scenes of Haiti, both urban and rural. Some captions are in English only, some in French only, and some are in both languages.

The Elite of Haitian Society/Photograph/1938/Courtesy Charles L. Blockson Afro-American Collection, Temple University/Pictured are members of this elite class of married men and women from similar backgrounds. During the period when the French controlled the colony of Saint Dominique, the free Affranchis or mulattos readily succumbed to the cultural hegemony of white society. They accepted without question the virtue of whiteness in both color and culture, growing to despise enslaved Haitians for their blackness.

Sous Le Signe De L'Unite Nationale/Courtesy Charles L. Blockson Afro-American Collection, Temple University/This uncommon campaign poster and photograph of Dr. François Duvalier was circulated when he campaigned for president of Haiti. After he won the presidency, Duvalier gained the respect of the Haitian people by improving the conditions of the poor and by attracting foreign business to improve the economy of Haiti. Later, Duvalier earned an international reputation as an oppressive leader.

The National Palace of Haiti/Courtesy Charles L. Blockson Private Collection/The statue of Jean-Jacques Dessalines, hero of Haiti's war of independence, is in the foreground. The palace and the statue are located in Port-au-Prince, Haiti's capital city.

Haitian Woman Selling Grapes/Print/Courtesy Charles L. Blockson Private Collection/Vendors of African descent have a long and interesting tradition, dating back to the continent of Africa. Shown here is a Haitian woman on her way to the market place with a large basket filled with grapes.

Haiti's World-Famous Iron Market/Photograph/Courtesy Charles L. Blockson Private Collection/Haiti's world-famous Iron Market is located in the capital and chief commercial center, Port-au-Prince. A group of tourists can be seen walking through the market while vendors sell their products at open-air stalls in the street.

VENDORS ON THE WAY TO MARKET, CAP-HAITIEN

HAITI'S WORLD-FAMOUS IRON MARKET

Haitian Money/Courtesy Charles L. Blockson Private Collection/Haitian banks and the government issue paper money or checks as opposed to coins for large payments. Coins generally are used only for small payments. Both the monetary paper and coins in Haiti are called gourde.

Sleptit Samedi Soir La Revve De L'actulate Culturelle Hatienne/1970s/Courtesy Charles L. Blockson Afro-American Collection, Temple University/Published during the mid-1970s in Port-au-Prince, Haiti, the magazine contains articles with information pertaining to political, social, historical, educational, and cultural life in Haiti.

President Jean-Bertrand Aristide/Courtesy Charles L. Blockson Afro-American Collection, Temple University/Jean-Bertrand Aristide, a former Roman Catholic parish priest, was sworn in as Haiti's first democratically elected president on February 17, 1991. As president, he declared that "all Haitians be treated justly as God's people. All should have food and shelter, and that all take pride in their Creole language and culture." In January 2004, on the eve of Haiti's bicentennial as the first black independent republic in the Western Hemisphere, one of Haiti's largest anti-government demonstrations included about ten thousand people who marched in the capital to call for Aristide's resignation. Ironically, the demonstrations occurred while Aristide was leading a restitution campaign to demand that France return the money that Haiti was forced to pay its former colonizers after independence.

BOOKS AND PAMPHLETS RELATING TO HAITI'S HISTORY AND CULTURE

Pour La Liberte 1915–1935, two volumes, George Sylvain, Port-au-Prince, 1925.

Efforts Et Resultats, Stenio Vincent, Port-au-Prince, 1926.

Le Document-Organe de La Libarire d'Haiti Et Euvres de La Pensee Hatitienne, Volume 1, Port-au-Prince, 1940.

Project de Constitution-Conforme a la Destinee Glorieuse Du Peuple Haitien Telle Qu'elle Fut Forgee Par Nos Aeux De 1790 a 1803, by Le Docteur François Dalencour, Port-au Prince, 1946.

PRESIDENT JEAN-BERTRAND ARISTIDE

Problemade Clases en la Historia de Haiti Lorimer Denis y Dr. François Duvalier al Servicio de la Juventud Collection "Le Griots," 1948.

Le VoDou Hatien-Rite Radas Preface Du Dr. Pierre Mabille, Port-au-Prince, 1945.

Le Document-Orane de la Librairie D'Histoire D'Haiti, Mentor Laurent Mrot Le Vendredi, 1955.

Avec Merisier Jeannis Une de Vie Jacmelienne et Nationale, Washington, DC, 1955.

Revolution et Contre Revolution en Haiti, Colbert Bonhomme, Port-au-Prince, 1957.

Le Marthon de Claude Confortes et Leroi Moko de Rassoul Labuchin, Reynold Eustache, 1975.

Jeremie D'Antan, 1673–1789, Martin Guiton Dorimain, Port-au-Prince, 1978.

Schema de l'Or de Jacmel Par Le Tr. III Fr. Leon Ph. Lamothe, Port-au-Prince, 1979. (Haitian Masonic History Orient de Jacmel.)

Diaspora-2Eme Festival de la Diaspora Africaine du Noveau Monde 5–15 Aout 1979, Port-au-Prince, Haiti. Message de Excellence Jean-Claude Duvalier, President of Haiti.

Les Decorations Haitiennes A Travers L'Histoire De'die a Son Excellence Le General Paul E. Magloire, President de la Republique d'Haiti, Preface, Edmond Magones, Collectionnlur Proprietaire de Bibliotheque et'd Archives Privees de Premiere Class, Port-au-Prince, Haiti, 1954.

INCLUDED HERE ARE VARIOUS UNCOMMON PAMPHLETS, NEWSPAPERS, REPORTS, AND OTHER INTERESTING ITEMS RELATING TO CONTEMPORARY POLITICAL AND SOCIAL CONDITIONS IN HAITI.

Manchet—Newspaper—January, March, July 1980

Haitian Patriote—Newspaper—March 1982 (Bilinge—Bilingual)

Collectif Paroles—Magazine—December 1981–January 1982

MHL Bulletin Information—Movement Haitian de Liberation—Magazine–February 1978

Asile Politique Pour Les Refugies Haitiens—Magazine–October 1981

Idees, Revue Interuniversitaire et Communataire—Magazine—Fall 1977

Natif Natal—Bulletin—March 1978

Haiti Liberation—Bulletin—December 1980

Haiti Report—Magazine—Fall 1980

Haitian Refuge Center—Newsletter—August 3, 1982

Philadelphia Haitian Community Directory, First Edition, November 2003

Haitian Cuisine/Courtesy Charles L. Blockson Afro-American Collection, Temple University/On display are several menus representing various restaurants specializing in Haitian American cuisine.

Haitian history that centers on the dramatic and turbulent years of the Haitian slave revolt is an important story about the determination of oppressed Africans to gain their freedom with armed struggle. Yet there is another history of Haiti: the cultural and social life of the Haitian people stimulated after they gained their independence. This final category includes information that gives a glimpse of Haitian life. It is diverse, almost infinite, and always informative. For example, King Henri Christophe established the first art academy in his palace; later, he killed himself with a silver bullet in 1820. His life inspired the American playwright Eugene O'Neill in the theme of his play *The Emperor Jones*. Haiti's Declaration of Independence was written by one of the country's early writers, Boisrond-Tonnerre. Well-known writers in the 1900s included Louis Borno, Price-Mars, Thomas Lechaud, Georges and Abel Léger, Jacques C. Antoine, Edner Brutus, Jean Fauchard, Jacques Romain, Jean Brierre, and Roussan Camille.

In 1943, DeWitt Peters, a New York artist, established the Centre d'Art in Port-au-Prince. Through this institution, Hector Hyppolite, Antonio Joseph, and Jean-Baptiste Bottex became famous artists. Other notable Haitian artists include Petion Savain, Luckner Lazard, and Vergniaud Pierre-Noel as well as Normil Ulysses Charles, a leading sculptor. Haitian music, usually in minor key, is a combination of African and Spanish music but is greatly influenced by France, Cuba, and Trinidad. Ludovic Lamothe is famous for his compositions on "Carnival" scenes. Justin Elie and Franck Lessegue also are well-known musicians. Most Haitian artists, musicians, and writers use the rich folk tales and songs of Haiti for their material. Haiti has a national museum and library at Port-au-Prince; both are devoted to history, art, and music.

HAITI AND THE THEATER

For more than one hundred and fifty years, Haiti and its people have captured the imagination of numerous playwrights. Books and playbills represent the theater section in the exhibition. The cultural impact of this subject includes Eugene O'Neill's *The Emperor Jones* (1921)—African American actor Charles Gilpin, as Emperor Jones, shared the great success of that play with O'Neill. Paul Robeson, who also received wide recognition for his performance, followed Gilpin. In 1928, Dr. Leslie Pinckney Hill, former president of Cheyney University in Pennsylvania, published his most important work, *Toussaint L'Ouverture: A Dramatic History*, written in five parts and thirty-five scenes. Dr. W.E.B. DuBois' play *Haiti*, a melodrama of the historic struggle in which Toussaint L'Ouverture led

PAUL ROBESON STARRING IN EMPEROR JONES

black Haitians against the French, was performed at the Federal Theater in New York City in 1935. Also on display is George A. Zabriskie's play, *Henri I—King of Haiti,* reprinted from the New York Historical Society, *Quarterly Bulletin,* January 1943. *The Revolutionists: A Tragedy in Three Acts,* published in 1942, written by Seldon Rodman, focuses on the lives of Toussaint L'Ouverture, Jean-Jacques Dessalines, and Henri Christophe. *Monsieur Toussaint* is a play written by Edouard Glissant, an award-winning author from Martinique.

ITEMS ON DISPLAY

Paul Robeson (1898–1976)/Courtesy Charles L. Blockson Private Collection/Scholar, athlete, lawyer, singer, actor, linguist, activist, and humanitarian Paul Robeson was born in Princeton, New Jersey, on April 9, 1898. As a scholarship student at Rutgers University, Robeson excelled academically and athletically, graduating Phi Beta Kappa. Robeson built a stellar career as an actor and concert artist whose voice and name were loved and respected throughout the world. In high school, Robeson participated in a statewide oratorical contest delivering *Toussaint L'Ouverture* by Wendell Phillips.

While on tour in Russia in 1935, Robeson met Sergei Eisenstein. The celebrated film director wanted Robeson to act in his film based on the Haitian Revolution tentatively entitled, *Black Majesty.* Earlier, during the mid-1920s, Robeson performed on the stage in *The Emperor Jones.* Eugene O'Neill, one of America's greatest dramatists, wrote the play. The play was based on Henri Christophe, king of Haiti. In 1933, Robeson once again performed *The Emperor Jones* in the movie version of the play. Two years later, while living in London, Robeson accepted an offer from C.L.R. James to portray Toussaint L'Ouverture. Paul Robeson died in Philadelphia in 1976.

Langston Hughes (1902–1967)/Courtesy Charles L. Blockson Afro-American Collection, Temple University/James Langston Hughes was born in 1902 in Joplin, Missouri. He was a poet, author, anthropologist, librettist, songwriter, columnist, translator, and founder of theaters. Hughes achieved fame as a poet during the burgeoning of the arts known as the Harlem Renaissance during the 1920s. A prolific writer, Hughes wrote numerous books, and a number of works were related to Haiti, a country he loved and visited throughout his life. Shown here is a children's

ARNA BONTEMPS AND LANGSTON HUGHES

book, *Popo and Fifina*, co-authored by his friend Arna Bontemps, published in 1932. The names Popo and Fifina belong to a young Haitian boy and girl. "Simplicity, realism, a poetic charm—all these appeal to small children who will meet Haiti for the first time in this book." During the summer of 1931, Hughes began to write a play based on the life of Dessalines called *The Bravest of the Brave*. He subsequently titled the drama *Drums of Haiti*. A few years later, he collaborated with African American composer William Grant Still and revised and renamed it again as the libretto for his opera *Troubled Island*.

Troubled Island—An Opera in Three Acts by William Grant Still/Libretto by Langston Hughes, New York (1949)/Langston Hughes inscribed this copy.

Josephine Baker (1906–1975)/Courtesy Charles L. Blockson Private Collection/Born in Missouri, 1906, Josephine Baker captivated Paris like a storm during the Jazz Age of the 1920s. She became a legend in her lifetime. Early in her career, she lived in Philadelphia a short time where she was married. During the mid-1930s, she appeared in a movie called "ZouZou." In the movie's hit song, "Haiti," a feathered Josephine sits on a swing in a giant birdcage.

Justin Elie Original Composition with a Haitian Background Sheet Music, Boston, 1921/Courtesy Charles L. Blockson Private Collection

Katherine Dunham and the Music of Haiti/Courtesy Charles L. Blockson Private Collection/Dancer, author, choreographer, school founder, and anthropologist, Katherine Dunham was born in 1909 in Chicago, Illinois. Best known as a popular and widely acclaimed dancer, her dance troupe performed on stages throughout the world in the 1940s and 1950s. She wrote a doctoral thesis on the dances of Haiti that was published in Spanish, French, and English and later published with the title, "Dances of Haiti." Shown here is her book *Island Possessed*, published in 1969; her recording entitled *Katherine Dunham and the Ensemble Afro Caribbean: Songs and Rhythms Associated with Caribbean Music*; and the record album, *Caribe*—calypso songs sung by Josephine Premice who also danced with Katherine Dunham's internationally known dance troupe. Two record albums, *Voodoo—Authentic Music of Haiti* and *Folk Music of Haiti*, represent Haitian music.

HAITIAN LITERATURE AND CULTURE: PAST AND PRESENT
ITEMS ON DISPLAY

Carib Queens/Boston, 1935/By Charles E. Waterman/Courtesy Charles L. Blockson Private Collection/This novel, written by African American writer Charles E. Waterman, is a spirited and interesting portrayal of the lives of three women born in the Caribbean islands who became queens: Josephine, wife of Napoleon; Defilee, wife of Dessalines; and Marie-Louise, wife of Christophe.

Temoignages Sur La Vie Et L'oevre du Dr. Jean Price-Mars, 1956/By Dr. Price-Mars/Courtesy Charles L. Blockson Private Collection/*Temoignages* is an important book written brilliantly by a well-respected Haitian anthropologist, Dr. Price-Mars, who also wrote a seminal book on Haitian folklore. In 1926, Price-Mars published the infamous book *Ainsi Parla L'Oncle* (translated *This Is What Uncle Said*). This book describes Haitian peasants' ways of life.

Arnaud "Arna" W. Bontemps (1902–1973)/*Drums at Dusk*, 1939/Courtesy Charles L. Blockson Afro-American Collection, Temple University/Born in 1902 in Alexander, Louisiana, Arna Bontemps emerged during the Harlem Renaissance. He wrote, edited, and compiled numerous books in various genres for nearly sixty years. The featured novel is a story of the Haitian Revolution.

Dr. William Edward Burghardt DuBois (1868–1963)/Print/Courtesy Charles L. Blockson Private Collection/Born in Massachusetts, 1868, Dr. W.E.B. DuBois was a scholar, educator, historian, author, poet, sociologist, and political activist. DuBois has been called the premier architect of the modern civil rights movement. His grand-father Alexander was born of freed parents in Haiti. He left Haiti during the presidency of Jean-Pierre Boyer. DuBois was a founding member of the National Association for the Advancement of Colored People (NAACP) in 1909 while serving as editor of *Crisis Magazine,* the official publication of the NAACP. DuBois wrote numer-ous articles on Haiti.

James Weldon Johnson (1871–1938)/Print/Courtesy Charles L. Blockson Private Collection/Born in 1871 in Jack-sonville, Florida, James Weldon Johnson was a teacher, lyricist, author, poet, and civil rights activist. His father was born a free man of mixed ancestry. His mother was of French and Haitian ancestry. Between 1904 and 1912, Johnson held two diplomatic posts. He served as United States Consul in Nicaragua and later in Venezuela. Dur-ing the 1920s, Johnson served twice as acting secretary of the NAACP. During his first term as executive secretary, he visited Haiti to investigate reports of harsh treatment of that country's citizens following occupation by the United States Marines in 1915. Johnson deemed that imperialism by the United States government was unjustified. He col-laborated with his brother John Rosamond John-son in writing "Lift Every Voice and Sing," known as the Negro national anthem.

ZORA NEALE HURSTON

Tell My Horse: Voodoo Life in Haiti-Jamaica, 1938/By Zora Neale Hurston/Courtesy Charles L. Blockson Afro-American Collection, Temple University/Born in Florida, 1891, Zora Neale Hurston was a major writer during the Harlem Renaissance as well as a novelist, folklorist, anthropologist, and dramatist. Hurston's inter-est in and study of black folklore throughout the African Diaspora shaped her entire career as an essayist and creative writer. In *Tell My Horse*, Hurston gives a highly poetic account of Haiti's history and describes Voodoo as a legit-imate sophisticated religion and "a religion of creation and life." Hurston writes that she par-ticipated in Voodoo ceremonies and that she was invited by a Haitian friend, Dr. Ruby Leon, director-general of Services d'Hygiene to travel to a government hospital to investigate the appearance of an apparent zombie.

The Black Jacobins/New York, 1963/By C.L.R. James/Courtesy Charles L. Blockson Afro-American Collection, Temple University/Born in Trinidad in 1901, C.L.R. James was one of the twentieth century's most influential scholars. As the author of the influential book *The Black Jacobins,* the story of Toussaint L'Ouverture and the most successful slave revolt since that of Spartacus, James is widely rec-ognized as a premier scholar of slave revolts.

Life in a Haitian Valley/By Dr. Melville J. Herskovits, 1937/Courtesy Charles L. Blockson Afro-American Collec-tion, Temple University/Dr. Melville J. Herskovits was a former professor of anthropology at Northwestern Uni-versity in Chicago, Illinois. Long considered a classic study of Haitian culture, *Life in a Haitian Valley* discusses the African and French origins of Haitian customs. Herskovits also describes the daily life and religious beliefs and analyzes the attitude of Haitians toward the world.

Masters of the Dew/Courtesy Charles L. Blockson Afro-American Collection, Temple University/Jacques Roumain, one of Haiti's most distinguished men of letters, was born in Port-au-Prince. He traveled and studied in Europe, the United States, Martinique, Cuba, and Mexico. Roumain became director of the Haitian Department of the Interior and founded the Bureau of Ethnology of Haiti. His health undermined by imprisonment, Roumain died in 1944. In *Masters of the Dew*, Roumain retained the real rhythm and naturally poetic gentle speech of the Haitian peasant. *Masters of the Dew* was translated from French to English by two of Roumain's African American friends, writers and poets Langston Hughes and Mercer Cook.

Assaut A La Nuit, Poemes, Roussan/Port-au-Prince, 1940/Inscribed copy by Roussan Camille to Marian Anderson, Philadelphia's internationally known concert singer while she was singing in Haiti, April 1950.

The Beast of the Haitian Hills [a novel]/By Philippe Marcelin and Pierre Marcelin. Translated from the French *La Bete du Musseau* by Peter C. Rhodes, New York (1946).

Lydia Bailey, 1947/By Kenneth Roberts/The novel is based on Haiti during the Revolution led by Toussaint L'Ouverture and Jean-Jacques Dessalines. When the novel was made into film, it became a popular theater attraction.

Le Devenir du Creole Hatien Conference Prononcee Au Pavillon Des Beau Arts Le 7 Aout 1952/Organized by Michelson Paul Hyppolite, Port-au-Prince, Haiti, 1952/The program booklet contains several poems by Haitian poets.

Sorte Sorglose Haite/Aage Krarup Nielsen, Gyldendal, Denmark, 1956/Written in French and Danish, *Sorte Sorglose* is essentially a book of stories pertaining to Haiti's history and culture.

The Comedians, 1965/By Graham Greene/A novel written by popular British author Graham Greene alternates between comedy, irony, and grim violence. Greene weaves his characters based upon real people during the presidency of François Duvalier. Greene called Haiti a "nightmare republic." In the state-owned newspaper *Le Main*, Duvalier dismissed the novel in scathing terms. Greene and his novel were banned from Haiti. A film based on the novel was shot in Dahomey, West Africa (now Benin), and was also banned. Several African American actors, including Roscoe Lee Browne, Raymond St. Jacques, and Cicely Tyson, appeared in the film, along with Elizabeth Taylor.

The Wedding at Port-au-Prince, 1984/By Hans Christoph Buch/This novel by Hans Christoph Buch is a sparkling narrative set against the background of turbulent Haiti during the time of Napoleon and Toussaint L'Ouverture.

La Danseuse Exotique, Precede de Protocole Ignifuge (Poems)/Port-au-Prince, 1987/Courtesy Charles L. Blockson Afro-American Collection, Temple University/St. Jonhon Kauss was in Haiti in 1958. Kauss and his brother, St. Valentin Kauss, were both poets and publishers and are credited with founding the literary school "Surpluralisme." They reside in Canada and have published a number of books of poetry.

Black Poetry in Blank Verses/Poesie Noire en Vers Blancs, 1991/Courtesy Charles L. Blockson Afro-American Collection, Temple University/This text is written in English, French, and Haitian Creole. The author, Jacques R. Georges, was born in Port-au-Prince, Haiti, and immigrated to the United States.

An Aroma of Coffee/Ontario, Canada, 1991/Dany Laferriere/Courtesy Charles L. Blockson Afro-American Collection, Temple University/Born in Port-au-Prince, Haiti, Dany Laferriere practiced journalism under President François

Duvalier. When his colleague was found murdered by the roadside, he went into exile in Canada in 1978. He lived in Montreal, Canada, and Miami, Florida.

Apertrue-Haiti: Feeding the Spirit, 1992/Courtesy Charles L. Blockson Afro-American Collection, Temple University/This book contains both written texts and photographs pertaining to modern Haitian life and culture. Elizabeth McAlister, one of the contributing authors, writes: "Haiti is truly the most singular, most charming, nightmarish, sweet, heartbreaking and altogether different country in the Western Hemisphere. Beset by disease, hunger, exploitation, and violence, Haitians not only endure but create."

Krik? Krak!/New York, 1995/By Edwidge Danticat/Edwidge Danticat was born in Haiti in 1969. She came to the United States when she was twelve years old and published her first writings in English two years later. She holds a degree in French literature from Barnard College and a Master of Fine Arts from Brown University. Her short stories have appeared in twenty-five periodicals. She has awards from the *Caribbean Writer, Seventeen,* and *Essence* magazines.

The Heart of Haiti/Photographs/By Andrea Baldeck, 1996/Courtesy of Charles L. Blockson Afro-American Collection, Temple University/Dedicated to the people of the Artibonite Valley.

HAITIAN ART BOOKS AND ARTISTS

That people of African descent could excel in the European and American art forms was firmly established in seventeenth-century Spain by the success of Juan de Pareja, an enslaved apprentice and pupil of Velasquez. Many of Pareja's works were of such high quality that they were mistakenly accepted as Velasquez's own and hung in the great museums and mansions in Europe. From the earliest days of enslavement to the present time, Haitian artists have made invaluable contributions to the country's cultural life as well as having had great influence beyond its borders. Enslaved Africans taken to Saint Dominique were mostly inhabitants of West Africa where the arts had developed into a high degree of sophistication. Some of the qualities that served to refine the arts survived the trip to the colonies and provided Haitian artists with their unique art, a blend of African and French cultures. From the mid-1940s, with the discovery of Hector Hyppolite and Philome Obin, to present time, with artists such as Saint-Soleil, Andre Pierre, and Lafortune Felix, three of Haiti's greatest artists who were first Houngans (Voodoo priests), Haitian art has been a wonder to the world. Albert Mangones, a famous Haitian painter, sculptor, and architect, created *The Unknown Maroon*, symbolizing Haiti's fight for freedom.

Shown in this exhibition are several paintings that represent the simplicity of everyday Haitian life from the private collections of Charles L. Blockson, Picard and Sharon Losier, the African American Museum in Philadelphia, and other contributors.

GEORGES LIAUTAUD'S IRON WORK SCULPTURE

ITEMS ON DISPLAY

Georges Liautaud (1899–1991)/Courtesy Paul and Laura Keene/Born in 1899 in Croix-des-Bouquets, artist Georges Liautaud was a blacksmith, which undoubtedly explains the choice of iron as his medium of expression. DeWitt Peters discovered him in 1953 through the crosses he had made that graced the cemetery of his hometown. Paul Keene, a nationally known Philadelphia artist who was studying and painting in Haiti in 1953, purchased this rare iron sculpture (above) from Liautaud. His work is world-renowned and sought after, and his creations vary from the abstract to the figurative, steeped in Voodoo traditions.

Frederick Massiah (1886–1975)/Bust, 1927/By Normil Ulysses Charles/Courtesy the African American Historical and Cultural Museum, Philadelphia, Pennsylvania/Shown is a bust of Frederick Massiah, a Philadelphia engineer and specialist in the use of reinforced concrete. A leading sculptor in Haiti sculpted Massiah's bust. Massiah's wife, Edith, was born in Haiti. His son Louis, executive director of Scribe Video Center in Philadelphia, Pennsylvania, is an award-winning video producer who is currently producing a documentary on Haitian history. His daughter, Frederica Massiah-Jackson, is president judge in the Philadelphia Court of Common Pleas.

Ulrick Jean-Pierre/Courtesy Charles L. Blockson Private Collection/Ulrick Jean-Pierre is a renowned Haitian-born painter who lives in New Orleans. He is known for his provocative paintings of Haitian historical events. Included in this exhibition are the following reproductions of his works in color: General Toussaint L'Ouverture (issuing the first Constitution of Saint Dominique, Haiti, 1801), King Henri Christophe and his architect Henri Barre, and the creation of the Haitian flag.

Morgan State College—Haitian Painting/Courtesy Paul and Laura Keene/Shown here is a booklet listing Haitian paintings from private collections from an exhibition by James E. Levin, Morgan State College, who organized the exhibition May 11, 1956. Haiti has produced a large number of artists whose paintings are exhibited in Paris, New York, and other cities' art galleries throughout the world. Haitian artists have been classified as either popular or sophisticated, depending on the training and the background.

Renaissance in Haiti/Popular painters in the Black Republic by Seldon Rodman, published in 1948. *The Miracle of Haitian Art*, Seldon Rodman, 1965.

The Saga of Toussaint L'Ouverture and the Birth of Haiti/Courtesy Charles L. Blockson Afro-American Collection, Temple University/A comic book for children, published in 1966 by Golden Legacy, illustrated by *History Magazine*.

The Naïve Tradition Haiti/The Flagg Tanning Corporation, Milwaukee Art Center, 1974/Courtesy Charles L. Blockson Afro-American Collection, Temple University/This catalog represents art and sculpture by Haitian artists. It provides its readers with a history of Haiti's imperial military medals and other military decorations worn by presidents and highly respected military officers.

Where Art is Joy, Haitian Art: The First Forty Years, 1988/By Seldon Rodman/Courtesy Charles L. Blockson Afro-American Collection, Temple University

La Peinture Haitian—Haitian Arts/Edited by Marie-Jose Nadal and Gerald Bloncourt, 1989/Courtesy Charles L. Blockson Afro-American Collection, Temple University

Toussaint L'Ouverture—The Fight for Haiti's Freedom, painting by Jacob Lawrence, written by Walter Dean Myers, published 1966/Courtesy Charles L. Blockson Afro-American Collection, Temple University

THE HAITIAN PRESENCE IN EARLY FOREIGN NEWSPAPERS
ITEMS ON DISPLAY

Les Reugies Haitiens a la Legation de France, from *Le Petit Parisien*, April 5, 1908/Courtesy Charles L. Blockson Afro-American Collection, Temple University

Troubles Les de Haiti, L'Executions d'un Francais a Port-au-Prince Supplement/Courtesy Charles L. Blockson Afro-American Collection, Temple University

Litteraire Ilustre, Paris, France, June 21, 1891. Showing blacks and whites before a firing squad of Haitian troops.

Le President Nord Alexis Protégé Par Le Drapeau Francais, Echappe Aux Revolutionaire/Courtesy Charles L. Blockson Afro-American Collection, Temple University/Showing President Nord Alexis in his carriage amidst a mob being fended off by Haitian troops. Colored image from *Le Petit Journal*, December 20, 1908.

Ce Qui Reste du Palais Presidentiel D'Haiti, Apres L'Incendie, Excelsior, Journal Illustré Quotdien/Paris, France, September 8, 1912/Courtesy Charles L. Blockson Afro-American Collection, Temple University

The Illustrated London News, February 16, 1856. Shows His Imperial Majesty Faustin I of Haiti in his coronation robes and his wife, Empress of Haiti, in her coronation robes/Courtesy Charles L. Blockson Afro-American Collection, Temple University

Frank Leslie's Illustrated Newspapers, March 1, 1856. Representation of social life in Haiti/Courtesy Charles L. Blockson Afro-American Collection, Temple University

Harper's Weekly, February 26, 1859. "The Revolution in Hayti."/Courtesy Charles L. Blockson Afro-American Collection, Temple University/Shows General Geffrard entering Port-au-Prince.

Le Monde Illustre Paris, France, February 26, 1859/Courtesy Charles L. Blockson Afro-American Collection, Temple University/Shows General Nicholas Fabre Geffrard standing in uniform leaning on his sword.

The Illustrated London News, March 11, 1865/Courtesy Charles L. Blockson Afro-American Collection, Temple University/"Sketches from the West Indies." Shows landing at Jac Mel, Hayti.

Harper's Weekly, September 2, 1865/Courtesy Charles L. Blockson Afro-American Collection, Temple University/ Shows images of Presidents Fabre Geffrard and François Jean Joseph, the Rebel President. The third image shows a group of male and female worshippers of Votaries, the Voodoo god, executed for crime and cannibalism in Haiti.

Le Pelerin, August 8, 1896/Courtesy Charles L. Blockson Afro-American Collection, Temple University/Shows a white Roman Catholic priest and a white Catholic nun administering vaccinations to a group of Haitians.

DR. IVES JEROME

Harper's Weekly, December 1, 1888/Courtesy Charles L. Blockson Afro-American Collection, Temple University/Shows images of the National Palace at Port-au-Prince. Included on this page are images of Florvil Gelan Hippolyte, the Insurgent General, General F. D. Legitime, president of the republic, and Louis Etienne Felicite Salomon, late ex-president of the republic.

Samuel Dalembert/Courtesy Charles L. Blockson Afro-American Collection, Temple University/Samuel Dalembert, a native of Port-au-Prince, is a member of the Philadelphia 76ers professional basketball team. On March 24, 2004, Dalembert was honored during Haitian Community Appreciation Night at the pre-game ceremony before the basketball game between the Philadelphia 76ers and the Phoenix Suns.

Dr. Ives Jerome/Portrait oil painting/By Ulrick Jean-Pierre/17 1/2″ x 21 1/2″/Courtesy Jerome Family

ABOVE: VARIOUS AFRICAN
PEOPLE DRESSED IN THEIR
NATIVE CLOTHING AND
REPRESENTATION OF HAIRSTYLES

LEFT: THE EXECUTION
OF FRENCH SOLDIERS

GENERAL JEAN-BAPTISTE MARS BELLEY

SELECTED BIBLIOGRAPHY

Bell, Madison Smartt. *All Souls' Rising*. New York: Penguin Books, 1995.

Davidson, Basil. *Black Mother, The Years of the African Slave Trade: Precolonial History 1450–1850*. New York: Little, Brown, 1961.

Gaspar, David Barry and Darlene Clark Hine, eds. *More Than Chattel: Black Women and Slavery in the Americas*. Bloomington: Indiana University Press, 1996.

Hannon, James Jess. *The Black Napoleon: Toussaint L'Ouverture Liberator of Haiti*. Yucca Valley, Calif.: Pacific American, Inc., 2000.

James, C.L.R. *The Black Jacobins*. New York: Vintage Books, 1963.

Nicholls, David. *From Dessalines to Duvalier: Race, Colour, and National Independence in Haiti*. Rev. ed. New Brunswick, N.J.: Rutgers University Press, 1996.

Rodney, Walter. *How Europe Underdeveloped Africa*. Washington, D.C.: Howard University Press, 1981.

Rog, Martin. *Night of Fire: The Black Napoleon and the Battle of Haiti*. New York: Sarpedon, 1994.

The catalog contains a number of rare books not included in this bibliography but are highly recommended and utilized for exhibition.

The originals of *The African Warrior* and *The African Mother and Child* are from the National Museum in Denmark.

The oil painting portrait on the cover was painted by Ulrick Jean-Pierre.